BLACK ETHNICITY

A

Conceptualization

of

Black Culture, Social Organization, and Personality

Ronald A. Reminick

**KENDALL/HUNT
PUBLISHING COMPANY**
Dubuque, Iowa

Table of Contents

Preface

Out of the culture of the 1960's in America emerged a number of anthropologists whose attention and research turned from the far-reaching regions of India, Africa, and the Carribean to the peoples of their own "back yard" who distinguished themselves by their ethnicity in a milieu of urban pluralism. Out of this research interest in American ethnic cultures came a number of outstanding ethnographic studies documenting the customs, patterns of social relationships, and the textures of everyday life of the members of particular ethnic groups. The political instability in many foreign countries and the moral issues of the Viet Nam War and the civil rights movement stimulated the heightening of interest of anthropologists in contributing scientific knowledge that would assist in the amelioration of domestic problems. It was in this context that a focus upon Black America became sharpened among American anthropologists.

These studies are empirically well-grounded, concentrating on the details of observation. The theoretical interpretations given by the authors of these studies are normally conservative, as they should be, since social scientists appreciate the dangers of generalizing one's interpretations beyond what one has directly observed. But, in the light of the increasing body of studies being published on Black ethnicity I felt the need to place our ethnographic knowledge into a wider perspective of human functioning. This perspective is highly theoretical and eclectic. It utilizes concepts from several bodies of theory including systems theory, evolutionary biology, psychoanalytic and clinical psychology, sociology, and anthropology.

I realize that those theoretical models chosen into which Black ethnicity is cast is a consequence of my own theoretical biases and preferences and that another writer could very well choose a wholly different set of concepts and models to cast a very different picture of Black ethnicity. This is the mission of science; to pose interpretations and to critique and refine our interpretations of human groups. This, then, is one scientist's position in the interpretation of Black ethnicity.

I wish to express my deeply felt gratitude to Susan Lees who was instrumental in getting me to launch this work; Sue

Roberts of Cleveland State University's First College computer
lab whose patience and tireless efforts at teaching me the use of
the IBM computer while writing this book greatly expedited its
completion in a timely manner; and to my wife, Evelyn F.
Castillo, my heartfelt thanks for an uncompromisingly critical and
perspicacious perusal of several drafts of this work. And finally,
I wish to express my appreciation to my Black students, whose
contributions, dialogue, and critical commentaries carried on in
the context of my Black Culture course added significantly to the
ethnographic content of this work.

Cleveland, Ohio   Ronald A. Reminick
December, 1987

PART ONE

ANTHROPOLOGICAL PERSPECTIVE

AND

METHODS OF INQUIRY

Introduction

The first two chapters consist of a general introduction to the field of anthropology as it pertains to our subject-matter. It is a discussion of a perspective, a scientific perspective that allows a very broad view of the human enterprise and provides a framework for thinking about and understanding those problems upon which we focus our attention.

Chapter I is relatively abstract and highly theoretical. I begin by proposing a framework for organizing our fields of view. For example, anthropologists see the world in a very wide perspective, i.e., we think about human beings in a world context. We also think about human beings within a very small context, e.g., observing a family interaction. We think about human beings through immense spans of time, i.e., over periods of millions of years. And we think about human beings as they exist at a particular moment in time. Hence, the greater part of this chapter deals with the evolutionary framework and the principles of operation, the mechanisms, that govern life forces in general, human beings more particularly, and ethnic groups, especially the Black ethnic group most specifically.

Chapter II is very concrete in that it deals with how an anthropologist gathers data in a particular research endeavor. Here I focus on the primary investigative method of the anthropologist called participant observation. And, to provide the greatest amount of relevance to our discussion, I draw a good deal of information from those anthropologists who have done fieldwork in the communities of Black America. In doing this I also point out how, except in terms of geography and culture, the actual methods and problems an anthropologist is faced with appear to be quite similar wherever he or she works.

1

In providing an anthropological perspective I do not elaborate an overview of the various subfields of the discipline, although here I shall offer a brief outline. The discipline of anthropology is very wide-ranging in its perspective and eclectic in the development of its ideas. The science of anthropology includes just about every aspect of the human experience. Physical anthropology studies the biological evolution of the animals that eventually became human as well as those human animals that walk the earth today. Archaeology studies the products of the human career; those artifacts manufactured from the resources of the environment that provide at least a piece of the story of the human enterprise at a particular evolutionary moment. Moving from the physical past to the living present, and functioning as a sort of "bridge" between the infra-human and the human, we find the study of ethology which points out both the biological and behavioral similarities and continuities between human beings and our nonhuman "cousins."

The major focus of anthropology, in terms of the numbers of anthropologists involved and volume of research conducted, is sociocultural anthropology, a combination of two traditions within this subfield, British social anthropology and American cultural anthropology, with the French influence coming into the American perspective primarily through Claude Levi-Strauss. The technical distinctions need not concern us here, suffice it to say that this subfield has as its focus of study the comparative analysis of specific cultures around the world. The study of a specific society is called ethnography and the study of the similarities and differences and the determinants of these is called ethnology.

Also very much a part of anthropology is linguistics which focuses upon the structure, phonology, lexicon, semantics, and patterns of change of human languages. The subfield of psychological anthropology brings into focus the field of personality and studies the interplay between the forces of personality, social life, and culture of a people. My own focus of interest is in the psychoanalytic and symbolic interpretation of culture, social life, and personality. Currently, the last two subfields of anthropology have concentrated a good deal of attention upon the symbol and its meaning in different cultures around the world.

No matter what one's subfield specialty is in anthropology, our guiding perspective, whether it is applied very directly or only kept in a distant corner of our minds, is the evolutionary framework and its attendant principles and mechanisms of operation, which provide for us an explanatory basis for the understanding of the human being in society.

I

AN ANTHROPOLOGICAL PERSPECTIVE

Anthropology, as a scientific discipline, possesses a great breadth of scope and depth of inquiry into the realms of human existence. It is a holistic discipline in that it examines many different aspects of human behavior and attempts to create a Gestalt, a whole, that is greater than the sum of its parts. In doing this it often reaches into the spheres of other disciplines such as genetics, biology, experimental and learning psychology, linguistics, psychoanalysis, sociology, and philosophy of science. Being in such a state of eclecticism anthropology turns to systems theory (Miller, 1978) as its organizing framework. Anthropology organizes its various funds of information and knowledge into sets of integrated systems whose functional relations with each other allows the body of the whole to function adequately, if not efficiently. The following four-fold diagram gives us at least a glimpse of the scope of empirical fields of anthropological inquiry as it pertains to our present focus of study.

	MACROFIELDS	MICROFIELDS
DIACHRONIC	Evolution of the species of race of sociocultural systems	History ethnic familial personal developmental cycles of domestic groups
SYNCHRONIC	Global mvmts. Internat'l.relations Societal systems Culture/Ethnology Ethology	Ethnic culture Family dynamics Cultural personality and ego-centered networks

Diagram 1.1.

As the reader can see the major empirical fields of inquiry fall within four general parameters. Macrofields refers to the "big picture" of anthropological study. This refers to the study of very broad and wide-ranging physical and sociocultural phenomena involving the human species, whole societies, and intersocietal relations.

The concept diachronic refers to a phenomenon occurring through time. For the anthropologist large-scale diachronic phenomena very often refer to issues of physical or sociocultural evolution.

The concept synchronic refers to phenomena occurring at a particular time; a record of what is happening within a relatively short-term time-frame. An example of this, with regard to the focus of this book, is the end of the second World War and the tide of African nations gaining independence; the emergence of negritude in Africa--the assertion of the value and integrity of African cultures, the responsive emergence of the Black Separatist movements, especially in the New World, such as the Ras Tafarian movement starting in Jamaica and shortly thereafter becoming international, and the Black Muslim movement which emerged in the U.S., spurred by Elijah Muhammad and Malcom X; and then the "Black is Beautiful" emphasis in the U.S. which was the American expression of the negritude of Africa.

The concept microfields refers to small scale studies within relatively short time-frames. Thus, in the diachronic frame we can list ethnic history, history of a family, or an individual life history. The listing of developmental cycles of domestic groups refers to how domestic groups, ethnic or familial, develop and change over time. And, with the synchronic parameter we are recording ethnography: the description of an ethnic culture or a family organization or a particular individual within that ethnic group.

Four general systems are implicit in this diagram: Biological, psychological, social, and cultural systems. The anthropologist conceptualizes these systems as functionally integrated, although in a very imperfect manner, so as to enable the emergence, sustenance, and maturation of human culture,

6

social relations, and consciousness. For example, a personality does not exist without its biological machinery, its information learned from the culture, and its social relations which ensures the development of the personality. A social group does not exist without its cultural resources to provide meaning and method for its adaptation and survival. Culture does not exist without a social group to communicate in and pass it on to another generation. And the human biological organism does not survive without its social group, its reservoirs of meaning, and its personal identity.

Systems integration depend upon mechanisms of adaptation. This is one of the more useful explanatory conceptual tools at the disposal of the anthropologist. Adaptation helps the scientist account for or explain the form and variation of the phenomenon under study. Adaptation refers to a set of conditions to which an organism, group, or species must adjust to in order to survive at a particular level of efficiency. This set of conditions is often referred to as the environment. When the reference is human beings the control over the environment may range from nonexistent, as in the case of the physical environment of geography and climate, to considerable control, as in the case of a person's or group's social environment. The greater the complementarity between the population and the environment the better chances there are of survival and development. It is useful then to think of environments as nesting fields where smaller environments reside within and are conditioned by larger environments. Such is the case where organs function within the environment of the body, the person within the family, within the ethnic group, within the nation, within the geographic region, within the largest geopolitical and cultural fields that influence a population.

Natural Selection
The process of adaptation is itself a complex of mechanisms of adjustment working in terms of the principle of natural selection, a concept that is central to the Darwinian theory of evolution. In terms of the evolutionary biologist, natural selection can be defined as a mechanism of biological and

evolutionary change "by which the individuals best adapted to the environment contribute more offspring to succeeding generations than others do" (Campbell, 1985, p. 506), and thereby, through time, change the nature of the population inhabiting that environment. The other side of the coin, so to speak, is that those organisms or populations that are poorly suited to their environment will have a much more difficult time in their day-to-day living, and this stress and difficulty will feed back upon their reproductive vitality thereby lessening their chances of sustaining viable populations in the future. This concept of evolutionary biology can be generalized further into the realms of the social and psychocultural life of a population, for what can be said about biological change over vast periods of time, i.e., continuous adaptation to changing environments, can be said about social patterns and cultural forms and personality changes over much shorter periods of time.

The theory of natural selection is a powerful explanatory tool because it broadens our basis of explanation beyond that particular phenomenon we are attempting to describe and explain. Thus, our understanding of Black ethnicity can be at least partially explained in terms of the larger environment of American ethnic diversity and the general structures of the American economic and political systems within which American groups function.

The anthropologist is not only interested in explaining the uniqueness of an ethnic culture in a pluralistic society, but is also interested in understanding those unchanging uniformities present in all human beings. It is often these universal attributes of human beings that help us understand the constraints that define the limits of change at any given time. These universal predispositions, such as our need to live in family groups, our desire for music and recreation, and our inquisitiveness about the world around us, are very often biologically based and become highly elaborated as adaptive strategies according to the environmental pressures a population of people find themselves in.

The anthropologist doesn't stop here in building a context for the explanation and understanding of human nature. The Darwinian theory of evolution places the human species in a larger context and so the anthropologist looks further to our nonhuman cousins to see what in fact we share in common with them, for we are all members of the family of primates and what we find in common with our nonhuman cousins we can assume to be part of our own inventory of biologically-based instinctually driven patterns of predisposition. Those nonhuman primates that we have learned the most from regarding our own evolutionary heritage include the orangutan, the gorilla, and the chimpanzee. One has only to carefully observe the behavior of the wild chimpanzee, as Jane Goodall has done for more than twenty years and whose films have taught us so much, and to see their grooming behavior, the play of the young, the hug, the kiss, the clasping of hands, the family relations, to realize that much of human behavior is not human cultural invention, but rather cultural elaborations of <u>primordial dispositions</u> that provide the context for our evolution, survival, and development.

I employ this inclusiveness not to emphasize the "animal" nature of humanity, which is often commonly and derogatorily assumed, but to encourage an appreciation of the instinctually driven patterns of predisposition to certain kinds of behavior that we all share in common as human beings; predispositions that we functioned with long before we reached the threshold of humanity. And further, I employ this inclusiveness not to play down the instinctual basis for much of human behavior by comparing it to apes, but rather, to heighten our understanding of and appreciation for the intelligence and adaptive sociobiological institutions of our nonhuman cousins.

This evolutionary perspective goes a long way in providing a meaningful explanatory context for accounting for both the uniformity and diversity of human behavior. The principle of natural selection dramatizes what kinds of behavior proved successful in adapting to the exigencies of the physical and societal environments.

9

I find it useful to break down the principle of natural selection into four rubrics: a) biological selection, b) sexual selection, c) psychocultural selection, and d) social selection. In my very cursory discussion of these aspects of natural selection I will employ a progressively narrower orientation, mainly for heuristic purposes. So, when discussing biological selection my orientation is, primarily, all life forms. The discussion of sexual selection is oriented to the primates in general, but especially, the great apes noted above. The discussion of psychocultural selection is oriented specifically to humans. And, the discussion of social selection will be oriented, primarily, to the adaptive patterns of ethnic groups of both traditional and modern societies.

Biological Selection

With biological selection we are referring to basic physical survival through adaptation to the physical environment. At this level maladaptations may occur either because of radical changes in the climate or because of the onslaught of pestilence. Radical climatic changes could occur when a warm region becomes suddenly cold, as, possibly when the six-mile diameter asteroid collided with the planet Earth creating a dust cloud that shut out the warming rays of the sun spelling extinction for many species of creature (as one theory holds) during the age of the dinosaurs 65 million years ago. Another example of radical climatic change is the draught and ensuing famine of East Africa, particularly Ethiopia, that gained great momentum in the 1970s. Survival can only be sought through either migration or massive international cooperative intervention. The onslaught of pestilence could occur in the form of an invasion of a deadly, or even not-so-deadly, parasite that thrives within the confines of the human body, or a parasite that invades the primary food supply that a particular population is dependent upon.

Human racial variation is a good example of adaptation and natural selection at the biological level. For illustrative purposes let us take just two features of race for comparison, skeletal form and skin color. These two features can be seen as adaptations to climate and solar radiation, respectively. Through the span of evolutionary time, sometimes measured in terms of thousands of generations, living in an equatorial region has selected for dark skin which provides much greater protection against the harmful, carcinogenic rays of the sun. The melanin content of the skin is a defense mechanism against such radiation, darkening in response to exposure. The hot climate of the equatorial regions of the world have also selected for a slight skeletal frame with tendencies towards tallness, especially in subSaharan East Africa. A tall thin skeletal frame allows the body to throw off excess body heat much more efficiently than a body with greater biomass on a heavier bone frame.

In contrast to this we could compare the light-skinned peoples of the world and note that light skin readily absorbs vitamin D and is a defense against harsh cold which was encountered as the ever-migrating populations of humanity found their way into the cold climes of Asia and northern Europe. Light skin is definitely a better defense against cold and frostbite than darker skin. Along with this skin color adaptation we find that the peoples who made their home in the colder regions of the world also evolved a shorter, heavier stature with greater body mass as an adaptation to the cold whereby the body attempts to maintain a stable body temperature by containing the body heat within the greater body mass.

An example of a biological adaptation to a parasite can be found in the sickle cell trait of West African Negro populations which is an adaptation to malaria. Since malaria infection, caused by the bite of the Anopheles mosquito which introduces the parasite into the bloodstream, can be fatal, and is often fatal in children, the mutation of the normal blood cell into the sickle-shaped red blood cell proved adaptive in resisting the flourishing of the disease by depriving the parasite of adequate resources in the blood cell to live on. This allowed the host to survive, but as we well-understand, there is a price to pay in form of sickle-cell anemia. Of course the migration of the population with this adaptive trait into regions where malaria does not exist renders this trait maladaptive and with no redeeming qualities whatsoever.

11

Sexual Selection

Sexual selection primarily involves who gets sexual access to whom, the nature of the offspring that issues forth from that sexual union, and the nature of the social organization and society that results as a consequence of that selection process. The most basic and important consequences of sexual selection are biologically-based sex differences and that primordial set of social relations among mates and offspring and relatives known as the family. This concept of family is often known as troop or horde in nonhuman primates and is the archetype or the social matrix from which the varieties of human family evolve.

One early form of sexual difference that evolved among the primates was the sheer physical superiority or greater size of the male. It is commonly believed that this size difference evolved because of intra-sex competition among the males. Since female sexuality was and still is highly valued by human males and intensely sought after by all normal primate males, competition for the access to females resulted in the physically superior males winning access and the physically inferior males being pushed to the margins of the breeding population thereby resulting in a higher ratio of physically superior male genes being expressed in the next generation. These traits of physical superiority included both height, strength, and mobility. Among humans a narrowed pelvis and a broad upper body created a penchant and ability for running and throwing, skills that females could not measure up to but could admire and value for what those skills could get them. But of course these traits could not prove effective without an intelligence at least equal to the other male and female members of the group.

One further factor to note that helped accentuate the size difference between the sexes was that males did not restrict themselves to only one mate. Primate males tend to desire, if not crave, variation and diversity in their mates. In evolutionary terms they tend to disperse their genes through as many females as possible. Therefore, it is no wonder that we find harems among several species of primate and the polygynous preferences of human males, even in monogamous societies. It ensures that

12

the genes of the most able males will dominate the next generation of their population. On the other hand we find a much greater tendency, especially among human females, to prefer a more stable relationship with a single mate at any particular time. This predisposition tends to ensure the security and survival of her offspring through the long-term commitment of a protective and concerned male.

Qualities of attractiveness are also important in the process of sexual selection. A few general examples common to both sexes include good health, relative intelligence, and a certain level of aggressiveness, especially as expressed in resourcefulness and problem-solving. General female qualities that are attractive to primate males include the visual perception of sexual anatomy or aspects of the female body associated with sexuality, such as the derriere. Males are also most assuredly attracted by a female's interest in them, for in most cases a female must first be interested before a male can gain access. And, in all human groups a male gains sexual interest in females who show promise of procreativity. It is universal among human beings that males, no matter how old, tend to prefer youthful females for sexual access (Symons, 1979).

At least as important, if not much more important, are the qualities that females find attractive in males. Those qualities that females prefer are much more relevant to family life than those preferred by males. Females are attracted by male aggressive dominance expressed with his physical superiority and at least normative or relative intelligence for exploiting resources in the physical and social environment. This trait of aggressive dominance may possibly be the most primitive expression of leadership among the precursors of humankind. There is good reason to find this trait attractive because it allows the male to use his aggressive dominance for her benefit. Extending from this trait are two additional features of the male character that are attractive, viz., his ability to protect her and her offspring and defend her group against dangerous predators, and, a certain caring he may have for her which is expressed by his bringing her food, especially meat, and caring for and protecting her

13

offspring while she is indisposed. Thus, females are attracted by, and often excited by, male power which is translated as a power to help create a desired personal and family situation which consists basically of assisting in the provision of shelter, food, and protection, and especially among humans, the accumulation of surplus resources, the manifestation of which varies from society to society.

Psychocultural Selection

Psychocultural selection became established about the time that our species Homo sapiens sapiens established themselves on this planet. In fact, the human level of existence is commonly conceived by anthropologists as that point in time when culture began to be invented and elaborated. Leaving our definition of the concept of culture for Chapter III, suffice it to say here that through some four million years of biological and psychosocial transformation the mental capacities involving both intelligence and emotional disposition arrived at that point where the animal became capable of symbolic communication, i.e., created language, and in so doing crossed over the threshold into a universe of reality that no other animal shared. We must assume that there was some measure of compatibility between the evolving neurology of the organism and the social system of family and society which nurtured that novice brain, and the burgeoning capacities of the emerging personality system which now functioned in the realm of symbolic abstractions.

A sample of just a few of those personality characteristics that I feel were critical in maintaining an integrated survival and developmental system for humanity included the following:

1. A high intelligence, relative to the other primates.

2. The cognitive capacity for symbolic communication and abstract thought. This allowed for the communication and the sharing of experience so vital in a) mentoring relationships, b) naming and classification, and c) the communication of rules and sanctions so important in maintaining a human social system.

3. A certain level of assertiveness, aggressiveness, and the drive for taking control.

4. Empathic sentiments that motivate for sharing, nurturance, and protection.

Social Selection
Social selection involves the formation of social relationships that are adaptive to the environment within which that population lives. If the habitat of that population is a desert, where the climate is hot and dry and the food resources are scarce and dispersed, the social groups will of necessity be small, loosely organized, and nomadic in order to cover enough ground to feed the individuals involved. The sex roles will be quite well defined with the men, built for mobility and strength, hunting both small and large game, and the women, attendant to the priorities of child-bearing and nurturance, digging roots and tubers and collecting fruits and nuts and preparing the meals of their respective families. (The !Kung Bushmen tribe of the African Kalahari desert is the best-documented example of this mode of existence.) These groups will consist of nuclear families and possibly an elderly parent or two when the season is dry and the food and water is scarce. When the season is wetter, light rains, and food and water are more plentiful, the family groups may come together and form larger populations for that duration. This form of flexibility is necessary if a viable population is to sustain itself from one generation to another.

In contrast to this example, a population that lives in a fertile area where it is possible to cultivate crops and sustain a plentiful food supply, a denser population is possible, and therefore, a more complex social organization is necessary in maintaining order and stability. Larger family groups prevail, the number of social roles increase substantially, and the population becomes sedentary, thereby developing ideas and rules of territoriality. This latter feature is emphasized since it is very often the case that in fertile areas a number of different

15

populations inhabit the same region; people of different ethnic identities and speaking different languages.

Therefore, these populations not only evolve social organizations that must be adaptive to the natural environment, but also must be adaptive to the pluralistic nature of the regional population. It is usually in this context that competition for scarce goods develops and this in turn spurs a development in a more complex political organization capable of warfare. Thus, the viability of an ethnic or tribal group in a highly populated region often hinges on its resilience to the social stresses of competing groups. The less powerful groups then constantly face the prospects of domination or assimilation unless the political order in power allows the survival and integrity of a particular group.

Altruism is an important characteristic of human nature, which is well-expressed in the nonhuman primate groups as well, that allows for the building of relationships into wider and wider social networks. The primate animal is a terribly vulnerable creature and could never survive alone. The nature of our interdependency is primordial and the altruistic drive is instinctual. Altruism involves a certain caring and concern for other significant members of one's group. At least for our human ancestors, and as well for our infra-human cousins, it was not just a "survival of the fittest" that was important. It was a certain reciprocity, a disposition for mutual exchange, which evolved into mechanisms that proved beneficial to individuals as well as to the groups within which they survived. This emphasis on the greater priority of the group in survival as opposed to the needs for the individual's survival was given recognition in 1964 by the British zoologist W.D. Hamilton when he offered the concept of inclusive fitness. This idea was given greater elaboration by the American biologist Robert Trivers when he developed the concept of reciprocal altruism to emphasize the significance of group members not merely doing things for each other but taking risks for each other; engaging in behavior that may actually be unpleasant but that contributes to the pleasure or protection or the satisfaction of needs of the other. We may assume that a certain expectation for reciprocity evolved among members of a group and was learned and passed along to the next generation as a highly useful mechanism of social selection which had important rewards for the individual members. One of the most important rewards was the formation of stable family groups. Reciprocity and altruism were important ingredients in the "glue" that kept people together and this helped ensure the security and survival of both the individual and group alike.

In contemporary modern society this form of altruism within the group is extended to a variety of other groups through the capacity to recognize and value the contributions that other groups are capable of. However, the pluralistic nature of modern society creates different social environments for different groups who in turn have more or less power. This differential between groups necessitates different adaptive strategies for survival and development. As we shall see later on, the modes of social organization of Black American families and communities are their adaptive strategies for their survival and development in American society.

Dialectical Principles of Adaptation

In conclusion to this section on the mechanisms of natural selection, I include a few more adaptive principles that will be of importance later on. Anthony F.C. Wallace (1961) conceived the basic adaptive problem of human beings in society in terms of a fundamental two-part principle: the replication of uniformity and the organization of diversity. Whether we are referring to the human biological organism or the social organization of a population, once an adaptive structure is achieved it must be maintained if survival is to continue from one generation to another. An illustration can be found in the very structure of the basis of life itself, DNA. The diverse elements of the DNA molecule must be organized in a particular way and the replication of itself cannot vary too much without serious danger to its life form. The organization of diversity occurs at the synchronic level of operation and the replication of uniformity occurs on the diachronic level (see page 6). The exacting reduplication of the biological structures of living organisms is

17

necessary for the continuity of the life forms. The evolution of human social life is marked by the continuity of adaptive strategies of social relationships that have allowed human groups to survive and grow. As biological and social life forms become more complex and diversified there must be ways to organize the various parts into functional wholes. The neurophysiological organization of the individual and the symbolic communication and role definitions and patterns of social groups are the adaptive mechanisms for the organization of diversity principle.

Another principle I see operating in human society, which is very emphatically expressed within the context of Black culture and social organization, is what I call the principle of centrifugality-centripetality. This is a dialectical principle whereby these two opposing forces become resolved at a higher level of operation (as elaborated in the following paragraphs). It is most clearly found in sex role orientations and behavioral patterns, where male and female form an alliance which develops into wider associations recognized at the family group. These two aspects of the principle are in complementary opposition in that their differences, oppositions, create something larger than the individuals involved.

Centrifugality is the male principle, the disposition to go out from a central position. The male is the mobile, outgoing, hunting creature. It is a universal disposition among the men of the world. It has its evolutionary foundations in the hunting instincts of the male animal. Man was a hunter long before he evolved to the sapiens status. Man is the hunter of game, the source of highly valued protein that replenishes in the breasts of his mate the milk which nourishes his children. Man is the hunter after territory within which fresh vital resources of food promise sustained vitality. And man is the hunter after females who offer the promise of carrying on his heritage in the generations to come.

The principle of centripetality is expressed by the female. This is the disposition to be oriented to the center. The female is the axis toward which she directs the members of her family.

The family group is the origin of survival and the source of the most critical nurturance a human being experiences. The mother-child bond is the most fundamental of human relationships and the family is that primordial and critical context within which the mother-child relationship survives and flourishes. Mating and parenthood are the forces of centripetality in which both the male and the female have considerable investment. Thus the principles of centrifugality and centripetality are in complementary opposition. They are opposing forces which nevertheless reinforce each other at a higher level. Their dialectic generates a synergy that allows their separate adaptive yet mutually oppositional forces to create the phenomenon of the family. As we shall see, these oppositional principles have characteristic expressions in the personality dispositions and the social and cultural patterns of Black Americans (especially noted in Chapter VI).

A final principle to discuss in this chapter is the principle of zero-sum. In an environment of economic scarcity and a poverty of power the zero-sum principle becomes salient. At the cultural level the principle of zero-sum is an assumption of finite good. It is assumed by a population that there is only a certain amount of good or goods available and that these goods are not easily attainable. Consequently, people are oriented to their environment and to each other in terms of scarcity. Following from this assumption is the feeling that what is one person's gain is another person's loss; what is one group's gain is another group's loss.

In Black society we find sex-role-distinctive adaptive responses to this zero-sum principle. In coping with scarcity, females pull together--centripetality; they enter into relationships of interdependency and reciprocity and form corporate groups that facilitate the circulation of necessary and valued goods. Males, on the other hand, tend to compete. They go out from their family groups to collect scarce resources--centrifugality; are more individualistic and self-acquisitive and form corporate groups only when they find it necessary to deal with the power of other competing groups. Now, these tendencies must not be considered in any absolute sense. These principles and patterns are manifestations of dispositions and influence, but do not dictate, the behavioral decisions that make up the distinctive patterns of social life.

II

ANTHROPOLOGICAL INQUIRY

The origins and development of anthropology are marked by an interest in and orientation to small scale, tribal and peasant types of society. The discipline was nurtured by anthropologists such as Margaret Mead who studied the cultures of New Guinea, Ruth Benedict who wrote on the traditions of Japanese society, and E.E. Evans-Pritchard who studied African cultures during colonial times. The above-noted anthropologists, and a host of others, gave anthropology a good thrust forward in its being recognized as a legitimate social science. Their methodology was holistic in orientation and generalized in scope wherein the scientist attempted to know as much as possible about the culture. The longer the anthropologist stayed the more was learned and the more focused the questions could become about particular issues the natives dealt with. The major categories in the mind of the anthropologist that were to be focused upon, included those institutions we are all familiar with to one extent or another: kinship, religion, economics, political organization, and patterns of subsistence--categories of institution found universally in human society.

Units of Analysis

If any study is to come into being the investigator must have some idea of what is going to be studied. This must be established on two levels: On the geographic level one must decide on who will be the target of investigation. This would be the ethnographic locus. That particular group chosen may be a matter of feasibility or convenience, or, that group chosen may in fact highlight some theoretical issue the anthropologist may have been working on for some time. The other level, then, is theoretical and deals with the conceptual issues that appear to be well illustrated by a particular group. There must be adequate complementarity between the real people and the conceptual issues employed. Elliot Liebow's work had its geographic locus on a street corner in Washington, D.C. The major focus of his study was patterns of male behavior in streetcorner social life. He wanted to learn how poverty affected men in this Black community. His theoretical orientation included the postulate that certain environmental variables cause particular kinds of social patterns.

21

Implicit in this theoretical orientation is that which all
scientists work with: the notion of independent variables and
dependent variables. Independent variables are those which are
powerful enough to cause consequences outside their own
intrinsic existence. Dependent variables are those phenomena
that are believed to be caused or influenced by the dominating
or independent variables. The hypothesis Liebow worked with
was that the economic conditions of poverty shaped very specific
kinds of social behavior and relationships among men and
between men and women. The geographic locus of Ulf Hannerz'
work was wider in scope--his ethnographic unit of analysis was
the neighborhood. He was more interested in the variety of
lifestyles of a ghetto community, more interested in gaining a
better idea of Black ethnicity, which was his theoretical focus of
study, though a good deal of the data was male-oriented. For
both Liebow and Hannerz and urban anthropologists in general,
there have been added methodological demands placed on good
scientific research. Early anthropologists going off to study
small scale isolated tribal societies could take the whole society
as the ethnographic unit of analysis. This is impossible in an
urban milieu. The urban anthropologist must, as Eames and
Goode (1977) put it, delineate their working area; they must draw
boundaries around their unit of study to make that study feasible.
This can be done by geopolitical divisions, i.e., recognized
neighborhoods, suburbs, or parks, or it can be done in terms of
networks. This latter method of defining a unit is called
network analysis. It is accomplished by the anthropologist
starting with one person and tracing his or her network of
associations. These networks will form patterns and the patterns,
i.e., the regularly occurring associations one has, will reveal the
way certain macrostructural institutions or forces shape one's
social world. Other units of analysis urban investigators have
used include the following: studying persons having a common
point of origin, such as in studies of ethnicity; work groups;
common interest groups; those sharing a common dominant belief;
sociopolitical movements; the study of a specific situation, such
as riding the bus or the elevator, waiting in line, streetcorner
conversation, park activity, or shopping mall behavior.

The social scientist does not work with just one or a few units of analysis. There are usually many units of varying scope and conceptual content. When a scientist works with a series of interrelated concepts or units, we often identify this as a typology. A good example of units of analysis that fit together into a typology is seen in chapter six where the units are of a nesting nature, the smaller units of social relations fitting into the larger, as a series of marriages make up an extended family and a constellation of extended families make up the church congregation or neighborhood. The typology helps us understand the functional relationships between units or institutions of society. It assists in providing a sense of a logical order of things and in this way makes a contribution to our understanding and explanation of our focus of study.

Tools for Data-Gathering

Since anthropology is holistic in its outlook and eclectic in its conceptual preference the actual methods employed in gathering data reflect this orientation. Anthropologists accumulate information in a variety of ways. We study the censuses of the population under study when available. If there are no censuses we may elect to conduct our own, for this kind of information yields a superficial overview of the people in terms of their sex and status differentiation, modes of making a living, family composition, settlement patterns and mobility, and other such census information. It also affords the anthropologist the opportunity to meet people, inform them of the research, and evaluate prospective informants with whom the researcher may have a long-standing relationship. We may also conduct surveys, asking questions of a more restricted nature around the focus of the research study. And, where available, we will study written histories of the population of the region. If there are no histories we may still acquire an historical record during the course of the study through the elder informants who provide oral histories.

There are also more restrictive and technical modes of gathering information. For example, the anthropologist almost always finds it useful to study a map of the region. If no map exists the researcher may construct a map showing geographical features, streets, paths, and alleys; settlement patterns, important cultural places such as the water source if plumbing does not exist, the government offices, the bars, community centers, and other places the people regard as important. We like aerial photographs if available, and if we have access to a light plane, we will take our own aerial photographs.

Just about every anthropologist carries a camera, sometimes two or three. People are often self-conscious if not resentful about their being photographed without their permission so this is a sensitive area. In my Ethiopian field research, I carried a simple Polaroid camera so I could provide photographs to the people immediately while using my other cameras for the more high quality work. For those who are fortunate in having the funds to purchase cinematographic equipment, filming of particular events can be invaluable. But, still photography does stop action and the researcher can make observations in a different way through still photos. Photographs help us study nonverbal language, for example. We can notice more clearly the particularities of gesture, posture, and facial communication, and can stop the action of communication intercourse among a group of people in order to study more intensively the kinesics, the language of gesture and body motion, of the persons involved.

Other instruments of data collection include the tape recorder, which is useful in recording song, poetry, and other forms of discourse exactly as it was given so that the researcher can subject the text to linguistic and semantic analysis later on. And some of us use psychological projective tests which allow the free association of thought in response to a simple perceptual stimulus, in order to gain some insight into the individual's orientation structure, dominant concerns and areas of psychological conflict. These tests not only help evoke cultural material, they also evoke unconscious material which may lend a greater depth of understanding, and hopefully, with a good sample of persons, we can gain a greater understanding of a larger group.

Participant Observation

The distinctive feature of the anthropological method is the use of the anthropologist in the person himself. This method is called participant-observation and is the single most important mode of data acquisition in the fieldwork enterprise. As the term implies, this is a two-part mode of functioning. The anthropologist must become a part of that which is being studied yet remain apart, at a certain distance, in order to make objective, descriptive observations. To be a part of what is being studied the anthropologist must become active in the social and cultural life of the natives, be they natives of south Chicago or natives of Papua, New Guinea.

First of all, the anthropologist must speak their language, the most important skill in deepening one's understanding and appreciation of native culture. With respect to Black culture, we cannot assume that there is nothing to learn from Black English, for as we shall see later on, Black English is very different from standard English and at a very subtle level expresses some very significant aspects of the Black experience. The other ways that the anthropologist becomes immersed in the culture is to become part of their social network, wear their clothes, share their food, engage one's self in the daily customs of the natives to the extent that this is feasible without impeding the research. Many anthropologists find themselves "adopted" by members of a particular family or social group and become involved in many intimate routines and rites. Although it is exceedingly rare, it is not unheard of for the anthropologist to marry a native. But, anthropologists must be careful not to get embroiled in disputes and conflicts that could jeopardize the study. Therefore, a certain distance must be maintained in order to preserve the integrity of that first of all priorities, the research.

The second part of the methodology, observation, goes a long way in maintaining the integrity of the research, for the nature of the investigator's inquiry and his or her role as novice in the culture and society of the people is a continual reminder that this inquiring person is an outsider. The participant-observer uses the total sensory and thinking systems of the self, so far as that is possible, noting as much information as is feasible. At least at the beginning of the research, we make ourselves into a "sponge" and soak up as much new information as we can handle without becoming overloaded, for the overload may result in culture shock which contributes considerable resistance to our data-gathering quest.

Many anthropologists take time out at the end of the day to record the day's events, for often the natives become uncomfortable if not outright resentful of the investigator taking notes while amidst their company, especially if the social occasion is informal. This note-taking or recording period may go on for three or four hours before retiring. And, many of us will keep a journal which details the more personal experiences and responses to a variety of fieldwork situations. Theodore Kennedy's book, You Gotta Deal With It, is a good example of a study that combined both the personal and the scientific results of his investigation of a Southern Black community.

The anthropologist, then, comes into a field situation with a modus operandi. This concept refers to the strategies used for gaining data. One of the first strategies to decide upon when entering the field situation is to settle upon a reason for being there that is understandable and acceptable to the natives. If the natives are educated and sophisticated, as would be the members of the executive offices of IBM, for example, then the anthropologist might consider being straight forward in discussing the nature of the research. But, the natives may be quite sophisticated and yet very unaccepting of the research project, such as may occur among a group of urban-based American Indians who are often very sensitive about the literature on their people. Or, the natives may have considerable suspicion of the work because they may be putting themselves at risk, not knowing if the researcher is an agent of the FBI, IRS, County Welfare, or a journalist for a common tabloid that could publish uncomplimentary material on them.

This type of situation is likely in urban research projects where the investigator is working in the Black ghettos of the U.S., such as Harlem, New York, Washington, D.C., south

Chicago, or Watts, Los Angeles. In any event, one's stated reasons for conducting research must be both understandable and acceptable to the natives and congruous with the nature of the questions asked. Two important rules to observe when conducting urban-based research is, first, never treat the natives as "subjects" under observation. The humility of the researcher is appreciated and the nature of the investigation is better cast as the teacher-student relation, where the teachers are the natives and the student is the investigator. This is certainly realistic since the anthropologist is learning and the primary informants that the researcher engages may turn out to be the mentors in the study. Second, the anthropologist should never try to legitimate the study by stating that it is for their own good or because it is going to help the community. There is an implicit superiority in this kind of rationale, a chauvinism that the natives may easily find abrasive. Nevertheless, the natives may be interested in what the researcher can do for them personally and be willing to engage the outsider in hopes of some form of remuneration. But, it is not wise to be explicit about what the persons may get out of it unless there is a formalized relationship established such as the salaried informant.

Gaining Entry to the Field Situation

The researcher should have a clear idea of the modus operandi, the strategies of data-collection, before the actual study begins. However, approaching the field situation also requires a modus vivendi, some idea of how the researcher is going to live in the field in terms of the day-to-day routines. One's initial entrance into the field situation is an important concern and must be thought out carefully before making one's presence known.

There are several options open for gaining access to the urban Black community. One can simply walk in cold, without knowing anyone, and proceed with chance encounters. This is not a highly recommended access strategy but can be successful in certain situations. Elliot Liebow walked into his street-corner society in this fashion and one encounter led to another until he was well-enmeshed in the masculine world of his social microcosm. Where the sociocultural or racial differences between the investigator and the people under study aren't too great and the status of normal day-to-day relationships are informal this strategy may even be preferable.

A more formal approach is to have official papers or letters of introduction to a group or community wherein an official person receives you and introduces you to the larger community. This may be preferable when one is going to adopt a more formal role which is part of the existing community organization and conduct the research from within that particular role, such as becoming a social worker in the community while conducting one's research. The manner of introduction should be complementary to the context of the situation into which one is being introduced.

Another strategy for gaining entrance to a community would be to be hired in a less formal capacity, such as an unskilled worker and then conduct the research from within this role. But, unless one is researching the job role itself it would be inadvisable to get hired in this way since the requirements of the job may very well inhibit the data-gathering task. Theodore Kennedy assumed the role of a waiter in his study and learned what it was like to be treated as a nigger in a white racist community. Kennedy's assumed role was short-lived, finding it somewhat overwhelming in relation to the research he was committed to carrying out in this small southern town.

Probably the best way to access the field situation is to already know someone who lives there and who knows the inhabitants. In this way one starts off on a positive note with some assurances of building a network of relationships conducive to building the research data-base. A warm beginning like this can also lead to becoming well-entrenched in the community by being "adopted" by a family for the duration of one's fieldwork. Carol Stack already knew a member of the community she was researching, and as she accounts in her book All Our Kin, her introduction into and integration with the members of "The Flats" was smooth and successful.

Living arrangements are greatly enhanced when the investigator is "adopted" by a family. If the investigator is single it is often possible to reside in the same household or very close by. If the investigator is accompanied by his or her own family, a separate household will most likely have to be set up. Of course, the research household should be located in the midst of the social life of the community if at all feasible. If this is not feasible, a household or apartment should be set up as close as possible to the field area in order to minimize the task of commuting and to minimize the possibility of creating an alienating status differential.

Choosing Informants

Choosing informants is the next step in the field-initiation process. Anthropologists normally rely heavily on the services of informants who appear talented in the divulgence of ethnographic information. The nature of the information gleaned from the study rests heavily upon who the anthropologist's informants are. Although the anthropologist learns in general ways through observation and interpretation a great deal of information, sometimes the most important information, will come from certain persons chosen to be informants. Therefore, the anthropologist must be judicious in deciding who shall be important sources of information. There are a great many "story-tellers" among the natives, often making up stories because they think that is what the researcher would like to hear, sometimes doing it just for sport, and sometimes doing it to protect someone or something. Therefore, the anthropologist must choose informants with established integrity and who have an appreciation for the nature of the work being carried out.

A general rule of thumb is to disallow the first informant who comes along and to be suspect of informants that eagerly volunteer their unsolicited services; ulterior motives may be present. But, no matter who one's informants are, we find that the richest kind of information, that which really provides the deep texture of social and cultural life, is that information that emerges as a result of personal encounters and relationships, and

29

not from asking formal questions to which correct or true answers are expected. Therefore, the development of friendships is important in the fieldwork enterprise. The caveat to maintain in the forging of social relations in the field is to make sure that the establishment of a relationship does not engender a conflict that could impede the research effort. We must be sensitive to the status and character of the persons with whom we are dealing. If the primary work is with established families one does not want to be seen spending a good deal of time with persons offensive to family members such as the "alley people" Ulf Hannerz was cautioned about by the "mainstreamers" in his study. If you are working primarily with street people you don't want to be found talking with people who are associated with the police or any other branch of the urban bureaucracy that could be threatening to street people. And, of course, the anthropologist must be careful about interviewing members of the opposite sex where the jealousy of a mate could create a potentially dangerous situation for the anthropologist.

PART TWO

CULTURE AND SOCIAL ORGANIZATION

The concepts of culture and social organization are among the most important concepts employed in the organization of knowledge in the human sciences. They derive their importance from their functions as two of the primary determinants of human behavior. Two other major determinants, of course, are biology and psychology or personality. The cultural geographer would add that the physical environment has much to do with the shaping of behavior in human communities. These realms of human functioning that we discern from reality are analytical distinctions--ways we divide up reality in terms of perceived relationships between the parts of what we are studying. The analytical distinctions we make between bodies of knowledge are identified as systems, because not only do we derive particular kinds of relationships between the parts, but we also recognize lawful principles of operation in the functioning of these parts in relation to each other as a system.

Furthermore, we recognize an interdependency not only between a system's parts but between the systems themselves. So, on the level of biology, the organism, we see the organization of physical parts in terms of intracellular structures and cell systems that form bone, muscle, nerves, and organs. The flux of the system, what makes it go, is its physiology. The psychological system, or what we recognize as the personality, is dependent upon the adequate functioning of the biological system. What we identify as the "parts" of the personality are more arbitrarily defined; are usually determined by the conceptual models employed or one's theoretical perspective. There is, however, general agreement that the psychological system consists of cognition, emotion, motivation, and behavior. Each of these categories of the personality organizes its own responses to the stimuli from within and outside of the body.

The point of the above discussion is to emphasize that the systems of culture and social organization are direct outgrowths of and vitally dependent upon the adequate functioning of these prior systems. Although it is common sense to understand that

31

culture and social organization do not exist without people, my intent is to underscore a way of thinking about this, i.e., in terms of systems operation; to appreciate the interdependency and feedback relations of parts and systems. It is this way of thinking that facilitates our understanding of the particular within the universal, of Black Americans within the framework of human society.

Chapter III is a detailed elaboration of the concept of culture. It is a concept that is applicable to any human group, i.e., it has universal validity, and therefore, subsumes all other ethnic cultures in the world. For this reason, it is also applicable to Black culture and places the concept of Black culture into a wider cultural perspective, which I feel enhances the possibilities of a fuller understanding of Black culture.

The concept of culture is delineated in terms of structure and function. The structure of a cultural system includes its "parts" and their relation to each other and to the whole, the latter of which is often conceived as the Gestalt. The "parts" are the cultural institutions of society. They include philosophy, religion, ideology, technology, and science. None of these cultural institutions work without the flux of language, the primary vehicle of human communication. These cultural institutions are in contradistinction to the social institutions of society which include kinship, economics, political organization, ritual, and the extra-familial care-taking institutions such as medicine, clinical psychology, social service, and custodial institutions. The last segment of Chapter III identifies five general functions of culture: the adaptive, pragmatic, expressive, explanatory, and mnemonic functions. These functions reveal the basic needs of human groups and the elaborated institutions of any particular culture are its formulae for fulfilling those basic needs.

The distinctiveness of a particular culture is a function of its ethnic boundaries. These boundaries are geographic, psychological, social, and cultural, and distinguish the "us" nature of a group from all others, "them." These boundaries are a

consequence of centripetal forces inherent in the structure and function of all cultures. In the discussion of the ethnic group, in Chapter VI, I consider these centripetal forces as boundary-maintaining mechanisms of ethnicity, twelve of which are identified. Those forces that arise as an inherent function of the system include geographic isolation and the sharing of a common history, language, religion, and descent. Forces of ethnic boundary maintenance operating external to the system include demographic pressures and balances between groups, resource competition, discrimination and political oppression.
These and other mechanisms of boundary-maintenance contribute to the ethnic cultural identity of a population.

Chapter IV focuses specifically on Black culture. For the purposes of a theoretical treatment of the subject, with which this book is concerned, I approach the problem of conceptualizing Black culture by identifying its elements or features that appear to play an important role in shaping Black thought, feeling, and behavior. I look at not only the concrete aspects of Black culture like language dialect, cuisine, music and dance and the like, but I also identify certain more abstract ethnic categories such as the concept of soul, and certain principles that give Black culture its own dynamic, found more in the lower socioeconomic strata of society, such as the principle of zero-sum and the culture of poverty.

Chapter V treats what I feel is the single most important cultural institution of Black Americans, religion. It is within this cultural institution that I identify some of the most important adaptive mechanisms that have contributed to the endurance and vitality of Black culture and social life. I initiate the chapter with a general definition of religion which I feel subsumes the most important aspects of Black religion. I then proceed to enumerate what I believe to be the major components of Black religion, aspects of its structure--ideology, moral values, mythology, music and dance. I then identify the major functions of Black religion. It is in my discussion of Black religion that I point out the interplay of the systems of personality, social organization, and culture.

Chapter VI delineates the units of social organization and elaborates a typology based on a _familistic_ cultural model, a model of social organization where personal relationships function in terms of sentiment and reciprocal obligation. This typology is elaborated on two levels. The first level is the _general_ level, that which is found in all human groups. Each unit is given a general name, e.g., the pair-bond, a form of relationship that is found operating in every human group. The second level is _specific_ to Black Americans; to Black ethnicity. This level stresses the _content_ of that structure in question; the values, ideas, motivations, and principles of social behavior. In this chapter, and also the following chapter, we see how the pair-bond expresses itself in a variety of contexts of Black sociality.

Because the concept of the "family" has had a great deal of ambiguity about it, anthropological studies of Black families and communities in the United States have stressed the importance of detailed ethnographic descriptions of Black domestic life. It offers a picture of the social and cultural reality of Black Americans themselves and we extrapolate from that information what principles and forces shape that domestic group. The task of Chapter VI, then, is not to provide a definition of the Black family so much as to illustrate the _range of variation_ of familial units that is the mode of adaptation to urban American society.

The relationship forms that are under discussion in Chapter VI are called primary. They are based on sentiment and role functions. They are what Talcott Parsons (one of the fathers of American sociology) and Bales (1955) called "particularistic" or "familistic" forms of relationship, which place a great importance upon the personal aspects of a relationship. This is in contrast to secondary modes of relationship which place the greater emphasis upon the utilitarian functions of a relationship and greatly deemphasizes the personal. Business transactions, political and bureaucratic dealings, employer-employee relationships are examples of the secondary mode of relationship; what Parsons called "universalistic." Since universalistic relationships exist outside the parameters of ethnicity we will not ethnicity is at issue we should realize that those problems of civil rights, discrimination, and race relations are all issues involving universalistic mores.

III

A GENERAL CONCEPTION OF HUMAN CULTURE

A greater appreciation of Black culture can be achieved within the more general conceptualization of human culture. So conceived, Black culture can be seen as an ethnic unit of human culture. In its abstract components, which will be stated in my definition of culture, Black culture is made up of all those elements that can be found in our species. In the same way that the DNA molecule is the basic structure for all life forms, so all ethnic cultures have certain basic elements in common. Thus conceived, Black culture is isomorphic to, i.e., a microcosm--a small world within a larger world--of human culture.

Human culture is that phenomenon that set human beings apart from all the other living animals of the world. It is what adapted our frail species to our (originally African) environment and helped build our rational and emotional intelligence to unfathomable levels of potential. Our ability to learn from experience and to invent ways of knowing the meaning of the accumulated experience of our ancestors has given us a mode of adaptation heretofore unknown among the animal species.

This phenomenon of culture, then, has multidimensional parameters. It has both macrocosmic and microcosmic dimensions as well as synchronic and diachronic dimensions. Simply put, the macrocosmic dimension refers to human culture in general, sometimes written with a capital C, whereas the microcosmic dimension refers to the ethnic expression of human culture, the separate cultures that particular populations of people create and live by. The synchronic dimension deals with the modes of cultural adaptation that the various peoples of the world employ in adjusting to their respective physical, social, economic, and political environments. It is the dimension of the existential, the here-and-now; what we find operating in the world today, e.g., like a stop frame a film editor would use to analyze what was happening at a particular point in time. The diachronic dimension, on the other hand, is the dimension through time. We conceive this dimension operating at two levels. The macro-level is that of evolutionary time. It includes the evolution and development of the ancestors of human beings through several millions of years, from our nascent beginnings in East Africa to the present day. The micro-level of the diachronic dimension involves recorded history (see page 5). For our purposes here it is the history of the Black people in America. Later I will argue that a great deal of the ethnic cultural history of Black Americans cannot be found in the civilizations of Africa, but rather, has its roots in the pain and struggle and perseverance of living within the institution of slavery in the New World.

A Definition of Culture

My definition of culture restricts its meaning to what is shared in the minds of human beings. Thus, it does not include the behavior of social relationships. Social organization is an analytical category separate from that of culture. I make this distinction because it helps us understand human nature when people do things that are not in agreement with their cultural orientation and when cultural change creates pressures to reorganize one's social relations. That is to say, culture and social organization are two separate realms of human functioning. In this chapter, a definition of Culture allows us to understand the larger framework within which Black culture functions. My conception of culture involves both structure and function. The structure inheres in the key concepts of my definition as elaborated below. The functional aspect is discussed from page 43.

> Culture is a system of symbols, widely shared in a
> population, learned through and dependent upon language,
> the communication of which occurs in a social context
> and is established as convention and tradition,
> functioning as an orientational framework for behavior,
> thought, and feeling.

The remainder of this chapter will be an elaboration of the basic concepts, i.e., the cultural elements, noted in this definition.

The Symbol

The basic unit or nucleus of culture, human culture in general and Black culture in particular, is the symbol. The symbol is a vehicle for the storage and transmission of information. It is a vehicle for the accumulation of human experience that is shared in a population speaking a common language. Symbols are both material and nonmaterial artifacts of communication that refer to other things beyond their own intrinsic significance. They are invented by persons and possess an arbitrariness of meaning that becomes stabilized by common agreement within the group or population.

The spoken word "Black" is an example of a symbol invented relatively recently, following the liberation from colonial rule of Black peoples in various parts of the world. The emergence of this term coincided with the emergence of the independent nations of Africa and the accelerated push for civil rights in America after the Second World War. The American term "Black" arose in response to the negritude movement in Africa which asserted the integrity of African cultures and demanded that the outside world respect the ways of Africans as they respected their own. The term "Black," then, refers to Black ethnicity. But, we shall back up a bit to roughly trace the symbolization of the word.

The spoken English word "black" has several levels of meaning. Just about every language has a word for the color black. Every human word began as an arbitrary sound that found common agreement through time. Through millions of experiential associations it became shared by a population and developed overlays of meaning. In our American context the word became a substitute for the word "Negro" which is a term denoting biology, race, and subjugation. The word "Black" arose to change the meaning of Black ethnicity. This term denotes a shared experience, both an historical experience and an existential experience, of colonialism, slavery, oppression and discrimination, and the ascription of a people to the status of the underclass. But, it also refers to struggle, perseverance, independence, and the seeking after and forging of a new identity; an ethnic

39

identity that asserts its own beauty and genius and validates those original contributions it has made to the cultures of the modern world. Examples of these contributions are given in the next chapter.

The basic component of a symbol is its information. The sum of this information creates its meaning for a group or for an individual. The more information a symbol contains the more meaning it has, and hence, the more symbolic value it has. Normally, the more restricted meaning is found in utilitarian objects, many of which have very little symbolic value, such as eating utensils. However, even with this example we recognize that a knife, because of its wider variety of uses and potential for harm, has more symbolic value than a spoon. In any culture we will find a range of meaning in the cultural possessions of a people, with some possessions having more meaning and value than others. In more modern societies these cultural possessions may number in the hundreds of millions and include both material and nonmaterial possessions. Traditional ethnic food and clothing are examples of material cultural artifacts that may have a good deal of meaning attached to them, especially when used on ritual occasions. Names, spoken dialect, music, prayer, domestic and jural (legal) rights, political and religious ideas are examples of nonmaterial cultural artifacts that vary in their meaning and value from one individual to another, but whose shared meaning generates the "glue" that provides the cohesiveness of an ethnic population; acts as a vehicle for a coming-together, as, for example, with a wedding.

Symbols function as vehicles of conception; they are the "engines of the mind," which cue off ideas and sentiment, belief and value, memory and experience, whose meaning goes far beyond the intrinsic and immediate meaning of the symbol itself. In any culture, symbols operate in configurations in the same way musical phrases make up a body of music. These configurations of symbols operate in what we call systems. The concept of symbol system refers to a high degree of relatedness between the symbols which are grouped into larger and larger configurations. Mathematics is an example of an aspect of culture, the logical level of meaning, which exists in "nesting fields" of relatedness. These symbol configurations can be identified as the institutions of a population: marriage, kinship, economics, political organization, religion, art, science, and recreational institutions, to note but a few. These institutions have their own ideologies and values and attendant rights and duties and are often referred to as the "subsystems" of a society and are more or less connected, functionally related, to each other allowing the society to survive and, in some cases, flourish.

Symbol systems, though, are highly dependent upon language, which is in itself the most highly structured symbol system. Without language very little communication takes place. However, human language encompasses more than words and syntax and the written forms of language. There is also the style of a spoken language, most often recognized as dialect, or more commonly known as "accent." Dialect usually reflects the area of a country a person or group came from. Black English is a distinctive dialect and expresses not only the origins and linguistic history of the people speaking it, but also functions as a source of identity and a cultural basis for establishing social solidarity.

Nonverbal Communication

The study of dialect variation is an aspect of the study of spoken language. But, there is a whole other realm of communication that is much less explored called nonverbal communication. Nonverbal communication occurs on several levels. One such category of nonverbal communication is called paralanguage. This refers to "reading between the lines" or discovering meanings that lurk "in the shadows" of the spoken language. More specifically it refers to the stress or emphasis one gives a word or a group of words. It includes the spacing of words and the speed in which the words and sentences are delivered. It also refers to the intonation a speaker gives particular words. And, it includes the context in which the utterance is given, because context influences meaning. For example, let's take three simple English words that form a sentence: I love you. Just stressing one particular word

41

influences a change in the meaning: I love you; I love you; I love you. And the context certainly influences the meaning: A child could say it to a puppy; a man could say it to his wife; or to his consort; or to his mother; or to his child; and one could say it to one's god.

A very exciting area of nonverbal communication is the language of the body, or what is known as kinesics. Kinesics is the language of gesture and body motion. How we use our face, our arms and hands, our shoulders, our stance and posture to communicate to another. The tension or flaccidity of our musculature is also loaded with meaning. And each ethnic culture has its own style of body language and its own intensity of kinesic communication. WASPs tend to be controlled, with relatively little movement of the body, contrasted to Italians who are quite lively in their gesticulations. Jews tend to have a low-key almost diminuitive gestural inventory while Blacks are more stylized, up-beat, and musical with their kinesics.

And lastly, one of the less explored areas of nonverbal communication is the meaning of space in relation to persons, or what the linguist and anthropologist call proxemics. Most ethnic cultures have their own implicit meaning of space relations. There are some groups, Arabs, for example, who normally stand very close to each other when it is a same-sex group, especially among men. There are other groups, such as Anglos, who maintain a certain distance from each other, even when they are very familiar or intimate with each other. Just notice the level of discomfort among a group of Americans in an elevator or on a crowded bus. I would guess that Black Americans as well as Arab and Greek Americans would suffer much less discomfort bunched together than, say, people of English or German ethnic culture.

Language, verbal and nonverbal, with all its nuances, powerfully shapes and conditions our thinking, our emotions, and even the perception of sensation. One has only to observe and compare the communication patterns among a variety of ethnic groups to see the distinctive styles that emerge with each.

Convention and Tradition

To press on with our conceptual elaboration of culture, the concepts of convention and tradition are closely allied. Convention and tradition are, respectively, the synchronic and the diachronic aspects of cultural institutions. By convention we are referring to a widespread agreement about customs, conduct, beliefs, and general assumptions about the world held by a particular population. Conventions can be as concrete and trivial as when and how to brush one's teeth, or, have the symbolic power and depth of meaning to move whole populations to do something in concert such as the celebration of important civil and religious holidays. So, there is a social component to convention which is carried out in a social context. In most cases an ethnic group holds to these conventions with considerable resistance to change because, first, they have been habituated to them, and second, because these conventions grew out of a struggle to develop adaptive strategies, through trial and error, with a great deal of expense of human energy, for working out a myriad of solutions to everyday problems which then make living more secure and predictable. Tradition is the transgenerational dimension of convention; conventions passed down from generation to generation, developing a feeling of security and strength through a sense of cultural history and articulated identity, and generating a repository of cultural resources from which to draw enrichment and fulfillment.

In contradistinction to this perspective, however, we must also realize that in a modern society with a highly technologized culture many traditions lose their function, their usefulness, and so new adaptive strategies and cultural resources must be invented to solve problems for which tradition has no solutions. As anyone who is conscious knows, we, as an example of such a society and culture, often create problems of greater magnitude with our solutions than was the original problem. There is a veritable laundry list of examples such as the machine technology which, at its advent (the Industrial Revolution), promised Utopia, but within a few generations of time brought with it the erosion of the extended family, rapid social change, and environmental pollution which became a serious danger to human beings and spelled endangerment and extinction to more than a few species of animals. Modern medical technology has enabled human beings to become much more resistant to organic invasions--bacteria and viruses--but we have also encountered problems with population density. New and urgent problems are developing with the role and care of the aged in modern society. And of course with our latest computer-based military technological achievements we are not sure the human species is safe from extinction. It is for this reason that the anthropologist looks to human traditions in a variety of social contexts in order to reevaluate the status of modern humankind and to identify those aspects of mental, cultural, and social life that are necessary in maintaining sanity and a firm grounding in what sort of life holds promise for health and welfare on a global scale.

Orientational Framework

The last concept to explicate from our general definition of culture is that of orientational framework. This refers to the way an individual or group relates to the world and the meaning that world has for them. It directs the inclination to behave in a certain way in certain situations. What can be said of an orientational framework in particular can be said of culture in general. Whether the social context is a situation with one's grandparents, professor, doctor, or peers, one has learned ways of being in that situation and normally understands unacceptable forms of being in that same situation.

This concept is very complex in that it refers to sets of assumptions about the world and the meanings built up out of these assumptions and the rules of behavior that are developed out of these assumptions and meanings. The orientational framework is often the basis for explanations and understandings about the world or a specific situation in the world. It operates with configurations of ideas and images associated with certain feelings and attitudes that have their focus on someone or some thing. It is often the basis for certain values which guide behavior and social action. The orientational framework, then, most importantly involves rules and sets of rules, better known

44

as codes and norms, which are the basis for the standards and ideals of personal conduct and social action.

The Functions of Culture

There are five primary and critical functions of culture which have equal salience at the levels of ethnicity and personal identity. The concept of <u>function</u> refers to the operational contributions that culture, in all its myriad of manifestations, makes to persons, groups, and to the society as a whole. The other side of the function coin, so to speak, is what is recognized as dysfunction or malfunction, and, of course, refers to ideas, feelings, and behaviors that are not healthy or are destructive in nature, such as, for example, racism.

First, culture is <u>adaptive</u>. The human animal, in its solitary nakedness is a rather frail and vulnerable being relative to the other animal forms. The survival of humankind rested upon the evolution of a mode of thinking, feeling, and action that engendered viability, the power to survive, for the individual and the group. Through human creativity, manifested in play and invention, experiment and social consent, through trial and error, learning and teaching, the human group generated ideas of why and how, and formulated methodologies and technologies to survive and grow in and adapt to their native habitat. With regard to American society, ethnic culture in general and Black culture in particular are the manifestations of adaptive strategies for living in a pluralistic society.

Second, culture is <u>pragmatic</u>. Human beings are very pragmatic animals, much of the time. The idea, method, belief, or tool that works is valued. That which appears to accomplish the goal and reward the person or group becomes part of the cultural inventory. The pragmatic level is situational and concrete. It deals with the minutiae of everyday events and the need to make a multitude of decisions and solve a multitude of problems and tasks on a day-to-day basis. Whether we are sharpening a stick or immersed in some activity that contributes to the institution of science, the adaptive significance of pragmatics reveals itself. It is the practical and utilitarian concerns that shape an orientation and behavior pattern as well as those more abstract ideals and values toward which more people strive than reach.

Third, culture is expressive. Human beings have an innate need and drive to express themselves. Persons may express idiosyncratic experiences, peculiar to themselves alone, or they may express experiences shared by others. For those who can articulate a commonly shared experience and communicate it to those involved, a cultural performance comes into existence. Certainly, all human institutions are contexts for the expression of human experience, but those more specialized for the carrying on of traditions of human expression are found in religion and ritual, painting and sculpture, song and dance, drama and poetry, and sport. And, in the world of the urbane, culinary art becomes an important mode of expression.

Fourth, culture is explanatory. The human animal has an innate need to know and a drive to acquire knowledge. Intelligent beings derive pleasure in this endeavor just as certainly as a child experiences the acquisition of language which becomes the vehicle with which to discover the world. We need to know why. Through language, idea, ideology, philosophy, belief, and mythology, and through science, explanations are provided by the bearers of culture. Our mentors offer a foundation of meaning and understanding that creates a perspective, an orientational framework, through which one relates to the world.

And fifth, culture is mnemonic. Inherent in human culture are the mechanisms for remembrance. Culture provides a reservoir of remembrance, a culture-history, be it written or oral. Through historic literature as well as myths, legends, and family histories, the person and the group maintain their sense of rootedness which secures their identity and stabilizes those values and social patterns that have proved and continue to prove useful and adaptive for that people.

There is a significant difference between written and oral history. Oral traditions often telescope time, collapse it more often than elongate it. Oral history often interprets the happenings of history through the experience of the present, and therefore, oral traditions of history are continually undergoing modification and reinterpretation. Of course, this also happens with written history, a good example of which is found in the new revisionist perspectives on Black history. But, whether oral or written, my conception of the mnemonic function of culture refers to any aspect of a culture that makes the past real to the person.

IV

ELEMENTS OF BLACK CULTURE

Black culture refers specifically to the Negro people of the United States. This is stated with the recognition that many people both within and outside of the Black ethnic group maintain that the concept "Black" refers to all Black peoples of the world, both in the New World and the Old, especially Africa. I must argue that I can agree with this assertion only insofar as the same racial characteristics obtain. But ethnicity is a great deal more than race. And I would argue that any social distinctions made solely on the basis of race is racist. There are others who will argue that not only race is involved but also the sharing of the experience of domination by a politically more powerful group. I will grant that the experience of subjugation, discrimination, and oppression are experiences common to many peoples of the world, yet, since so many African societies have won their independence over a generation earlier, there are many Africans who would not identify with the underclass of the world.

The cultures of the Negro peoples of the world vary greatly. Not a few Black Americans who visit Africa come home rather confused and disillusioned and promptly build a romantic memory of their visit to Africa in order to maintain their ideological convictions and a sense of their "roots" from which they strive to maintain their identity (many personal communications). It is my assertion that Black American ethnicity is unique because of its unique history in American society. "Black" is the identifying marker of the ethnic group. As a category of ethnic culture, Black ethnicity has all the characteristics of culture in general as explicated in the last chapter. Subsumed under these general characteristics of culture are the more specific features of ethnicity. It is humanly impossible to list all the traits of ethnicity simply because of the great number of features to identify. More importantly, because ethnic culture is a meaning system, that internalized ethnic system of culture will vary from one individual to another as a function of their family organization, church affiliation, education, and personal history. Furthermore, no individual can tell another exactly and completely what their ethnicity means to them, simply because so much of culture, so much of ethnicity lives within the realm of the unconscious.

Consequently, what the anthropologist attempts to do is identify those features that stand out as salient, as especially important, for a significant proportion of the members who appear to treat those features with a similar degree of importance. It is with this orientation in mind that I identify the following elements of Black culture. There is no fixed order of priority to this list because the order of priority will vary from one individual to another. However, I will maintain that a certain nucleus of Black culture does exist among these elements and I would suggest that they form a nuclear configuration consisting of soul, Black English, Black religion, and Black history.

1. Soul. The natives of Black America identify their culture as "soul." To have soul is to participate in and appreciate the Black experience. The concept functions to create a sense of peoplehood among Black Americans, in a sense, a "nation within a nation" (Gwaltney, 1980), a concept which defines the boundaries of Black ethnic culture. Even though Black Americans are a fairly heterogeneous group, ranging from poor ghetto-dwellers to upper middle class business people, from unskilled workers-- members of the "working poor"--to skilled technicians, professionals to criminals, those with no particular talent to those who are highly talented in one or more skills, in a sense, a microcosm of the range of variation of Americans in general, the concept of soul identifies the commonly shared experiences of all. Of course, the elaborated meaning of soul varies from person to person and from group to group, but not to the extent that the concept begins to lose its meaning, for the emotional meaning of the Black experience is powerful enough to encapsulate that range of variation of Black experience into a cultural identity that defines their peoplehood.

Joseph Washington (1971), reflecting the convictions of the anthropologist, writes that in order to know the soul of Black culture you have to live it, not read about it, for Black culture is known in the existential moment.

It is the shared sensibilities of black folk that one must participate in to uncover black culture, not just the written documents of middle-class Blacks who alone write or the institutions and structures they pattern after the white folk. The aural-oral qualities speak of black culture and provide the clear channel of expressive communication among black folk (p. 32).

Ulf Hannerz (1969) conceives of soul as an "affirmation of the black experience." The value urges one to "tell it like it is" rather than aspiring to pretense; to be earthy and to stick to the "nitty-gritty" of Black life experience. As Hannerz puts it, soul is not only an acceptance of the Black lifestyle and of the Black experience, it is also an "assertion of empathy" with the typical and common experiences of Black social life (p.145). The religious element runs strong in the concept of soul. The worship experience is the expression of the "heart" of soul. Washington speaks from his own experience as well as his research:

...Black people...appreciate the fact that Soul, the psychological underpinning that is indigenous to Black culture, cannot be separated from the emotional overflow of the worship experience....Soul is the supportive affirmation of Black personhood, of healing catharsis, of profound, ecstatic teaching about the presence of God. It is at once the inspiration and unification capable of getting Black people to stand up and get themselves together for the struggle (p. 46).

Hannerz recognizes that the source of the elements of soul is the rural South. To most urban northern Blacks their southern origins is recent history. Even though the residents of the urban north have not been northerners for very long, there does still tend to be a stigma attached to those southern Blacks who are migrating north, a stigma connoted by the terms "simpleton" and "bama" and well recognized by the informants to the Hannerz

51

study conducted on a street in a Washington, D.C. ghetto (Ibid.).
The concept of soul also includes the element of perseverance.
As Hannerz states,

> To be black is to be poor and oppressed and to suffer,
> and most likely to be marked by this, but to keep on
> struggling, successfully or not. Having to cope with
> adverse conditions is generally recognized as a common
> ghetto experience; in one way or another, it is a part
> of most ghetto dwellers' definitions of soul (p.146).

But, this definition has a positive ring to it because
"poverty, oppression, and troubled relationships are interpreted as
the foundation of an endurance which can only be truly
appreciated by others who have passed the same way" (Ibid., p.
157). Thus, a solidarity and a sense of cultural boundary are
reinforced by difficult experiences conceived as a challenge. The
struggle is carried on at different levels of social life: at the
personal level in attempting to achieve one's personal goals; at
the familial level with a mother attempting to support her
children or a man straining to maintain his family by keeping a
job that he finds deleterious to his self image and social status;
at the level of the neighborhood in struggling to maintain
freedom from violence and harrassment from both criminals and
police, or at a higher socioeconomic level, to maintain a
semblance of integration and middle class quality of life; and at
the national level in building the civil rights movement.

2. Language. Another vehicle for the communication of
ethnic culture and a marker of ethnic boundaries, is language
dialect and speech style, viz., Black English. Black English is
actually a very broad term because it encompasses a wide range
of dialects and speech styles of New World Blacks: the Creole
Gullah spoken in the off-shore sea islands of South Carolina, the
rural dialects of the deep South, the Black English dialects of
the northern ghettos of urban America, and the very
sophisticated style of the highly educated (Labov, 1972, xiii). In
the past twenty-five years, a good deal of study has been given
to the northern urban Black English dialect (Labov, Ibid.;

Abrahams, 1964; Bernstein, 1966; Cole and Bruner, 1972; Kochman, 1970), more commonly known among linguists as Black English Vernacular (BEV). Spoken by 80% of the Black American population, this particular form of Black English has been the focus of studies by linguists, anthropologists, and psychologists. BEV has been studied for the folklore and cultural themes that are expressed in BEV texts. It has been studied for its lexical inventory and its syntax. BEV has been studied for the psychological processes generated in the speaking of BEV, its relationship to standard English, and the learning problems engendered in a standard English educational context. And BEV has been studied for the way it functions in maintaining ethnic identity and personal intimacy.

It has become established that Black English, BEV, is a system in itself and reflects a unique historical and cultural experience. Therefore, the prejudicial notion that Black English is bad English should be finally laid to rest. Rather than attack this language style with the aim of replacing it with standard English (a disposition smacking of 19th century colonialism), we need to study it and understand it so that our insights will enlighten us about the cultural experience expressed in this language style. Nevertheless, it is commonly recognized by linguists, psychologists, and educators alike that Black Americans must be capable of communicating in standard English if they are to be competitive in the mainstream socioeconomic and political arenas of American life.

3. Religion. The religion of Black Americans, with its variety of churches, sects, and cults, is one of the most important cultural institutions, and certainly the most important institution on the community level of social organization. In Chapter V we shall take up a closer examination of Black religion. At this point suffice it to be recognized as an important element of Black culture. I suggest that it functions at three levels of operation. First is the cultural ideology; the ideas, themes, and image configurations that make up the thinking system of Black religion, which is predominantly fundamentalist in nature. At the second level is the social organization of the church community.

53

This varies with regard to the size of the congregation, whether the church is situated in an urban or rural milieu, and the nature of the leadership of the congregation. Normally, the head of the congregation, the pastor or preacher, is a charismatic person who has proven capabilities in bringing together and keeping together his or her congregation; whose behavior should be a model for others to follow. Most importantly, the preacher must be capable of moving the congregation emotionally and stirring them to social action. If the first two levels of Black religion appear rather abstract and could be generalized to a great many religious cultural styles, it is because the ethnographic detail of Black cultural style has yet to be elaborated. But, the third level of functioning of Black religion is the most important aspect: the level of religious experience. In sum, I suggest that cultural ideology functions as an orientation to the issues of everyday life as well as to the realm of the spiritual. Church social organization functions as a vehicle for bringing together the energies of a group of like-minded people in order to achieve a certain quality of life for the individual and the group. Both the religious cultural ideology and the social organization of the church function as vehicles for the achievement of the Black religious experience.

4. <u>Music and Dance</u>. A vital and integral element of Black culture is music and dance, whose dynamic currents have salience and pervasiveness within the Black cultural framework and beyond, heavily influencing the nature of American culture in general. For our purposes, I shall list the music and dance styles that I consider to be the currents of Black expressivity communicating the Black experience.

Gospel music, as it is sung today, is the product of the genius of Chicago's Dr. Thomas A. Dorsey whose contribution was received in the very beginning with disapprobation. But, the style and idiom caught on and became elaborated and ramified throughout Black America. It has become recognized by many as the heart of Soul. But, Black culture has contributed a great deal more musical genres. Blues and jazz have travelled far beyond our nation's borders, dominating the European continent where both these genres are recognized for their classic qualities. Rhythm and blues, Black rock and roll, rap and funky music are other musical forms that are recognized generally in the American population. The most important contribution in dance is tap dancing. Originating out of the slave experience in the infancy of American culture, tap dancing has come to be an internationally recognized classical dance form.

5. Cuisine. This is another important reservoir of meaning and symbolic vehicle for the maintenance of Black culture. The food of an ethnic tradition becomes distinctive because it is developed over generations, normally at a particularly important stage of history. It marks the formative period of ethnic identity as well as signifying to the people the nature of that historical experience. The roots of Black cuisine is rural southern poverty and the creative efforts that went into making common food resources tasteful and interesting and exciting. The foods that make up this cuisine include

> collard greens, mustard greens, turnips, and kale; black-eyed peas, chitterlings, ham hocks and neck bones; hog maw, barbequed ribs, pork chops, and fried chicken; fried pig-skins, grits, corn bread, and sweet potato pie; and fishing and hunting for small game with shotgun or stick.

6. Socialization. That element of Black culture closely connected to the category of education is socialization. This is a more generalized form of learning of enormous complexity, some of which can be elaborated in Chapter VII. Suffice it here to note that Black socialization patterns are a function of and an adaptation to the geographic, socioeconomic, and political environment within which children are brought up. The socialization process functions at three levels through the various phases of childhood and adolescence: at the parental level within the parent-child interaction pattern, at the level of the extended family where a great many more people are involved in the care and socializaiton of the child, creating a considerable variety of influences and sources of learning, and at the level of the

community where the horizons of the child's interactions are more problematic.

7. <u>Education</u>. Ideally, education should not be a distinctive feature of Black Americans, for the schools should be the arena of integration and the assimilation of the important features of Western civilization, which can be acquired without sacrificing one's ethnic identity or heritage. However, the ghetto school continues to impress upon its charges the character of a school system built upon the dynamics of a callous and self-serving bureaucracy in racist society. One would have to look hard to identify another American institution that could match the unintended power of the ghetto school, and other city schools as well, in alienating its youth from a major agent of American society. One very lucid description and analysis of the ghetto school can be found in the work of Gerry Rosenfeld (1971).

But, the ghetto school is only one form of institution of learning shaping the attitudes that make up certain elements of Black culture; it is the <u>formal</u> aspect of education. There is also the <u>informal</u> aspect of Black education, most emphatically learned in the Black ghettos of American society. This informal institution of learning occurs in the streets. Its lessons are the lessons of adaptation and survival and focuses upon the development of skills required to meet the exigencies of ghetto America. These skills include self defense, loyalty to the peer group, fighting, illegitimate modes of acquiring money and objects of value, verbal skills, artistic skills that may be learned in the community, and avoiding society's figures of authority. No clearer and dramatic documentation of this can be found than in Claude Brown's now classic <u>Manchild in the Promised Land</u> (1965). Admittedly, this picture is androcentric, the life situation of boys and men; but the predominance of the literature does emphasize this compared to the lifestyles and patterns of girls and young women which are more domestically oriented in nature.

8. <u>Recreation</u>. Another category of Black culture that can be noted is recreation. As with many categories of ethnic culture there is always the danger of stereotyping a people or their

culture there is always the danger of stereotyping a people or
their culture, and certainly in this case selective description will
focus more on the lower socioeconomic levels of Black cultural
behavior than on the middle and upper-middle classes of Black
Americans primarily because there is a much longer tradition
forged from the former level of existence, there are more
representatives of the former class, and there is a greater
literature on the former than the latter class of Black Americans.
Further, as is common with many ethnic groups, as a group of
people merge among the dominant population of the middle class,
the processes of assimilation and acculturation tend to dilute the
distinctive features of that ethnic group.

With this caveat in mind I divide recreation into three
categories: a) sport, b) gambling, and c) performing arts and
church activities. Of course, there is a greater emphasis upon
sport among males than females because of its sometimes rough
and competitive nature, yet this by no means rules out many girls
and young women who are even at times highly competitive with
the boys and young men. Neighborhood sports include stickball,
basketball, football, and fighting of one sort or another. In
school, especially in the higher grades and in college, running
provides opportunities to show excellence. Along more
professional routes boxing, baseball, football, and basketball have
all provided opportunities not only in showing excellence, but
also have provided paths of mobility for its Black players and
their families, and have allowed Black men to become significant
role models for Black youth.

Gambling within the context of the neighborhood is
definitely more characteristic of ghetto males, yet it certainly
does not disallow the participation of women. It is a popular
mode of recreation because it provides opportunities to access
cash through both skill and chance. Further, it emphasizes the
principle of the zero-sum game because its players are enacting
in encapsulated form what they are all too sensitive to in the
larger context: limited good and for whom one man's gain means
another man's loss. The gambling forms include craps, poker,
pool, and the numbers. The first three involve a group of

competitive men while the last also involves a form of competition but the players are more or less anonymous and among whom many more women are counted as players.

The third group of recreational activities include the activities of the performing arts and the church. Religious activity is included here because music, dance, and dramatic ritual are an important part of the fundamentalist Black religious service. Community centers often concentrate on theater and music and dance for youth as well as the adults of the neighborhood.

9. <u>Material artifacts</u>. This is a category of Black culture that is rather elusive and in flux, changing from time to time, yet significant in that at any particular time specific artifacts of material culture are imbued with a meaning that contributes to Black identity. One example is the almost larger-than-life Superfly image and fashion that dominated urban style and even found its way into a spate of not-so-great films produced in the Black idiom in the early '70's. It was characterized by a heavy dose of machismo, a high-style wide brimmed hat, and the large flashy automobile, all complimented by beautiful, high fashioned savvy women who, nevertheless, played out a submissive role with their men. In earlier times it was the zuit suit and conched hair that dominated the fashion scene. This material ensemble was for public consumption within as well as outside of Black society and functioned to advertize status and reinforce a feeling of self-worth by demonstrating the ability to access resources, to acquire objects of high value that were, and are, difficult to obtain. In the '80's in some urban centers the gerry curl became popular; a hair process that required men to wear plastic bag-like coverings on their hair for a time, often advertizing the process by public display because the process was long and expensive. It appears that a concern about hair, hair style, and hair processing is rather constant from one era to another. Negro hair tends to break before it gets too long. For this reason women place a high value on long hair and possess particularly strong feelings about hair in particular social contexts. For example, a group of women may admire the hair of one of their peers because it may

be unusually long and full. But, if this same woman is in the company of men, especially their men, they may experience envy and insecurity and may feel hostile toward this woman because they realize that the men will find this hair attractive, and hence, she will become a potential competitor for the attentions of these men. The hair pic, borrowed from the African cultural inventory, has become a fairly esssential utensil of hair care.

From the '50's through the late '60's and early '70's the large expensive automobile was an identity-marker. The white Cadillac of the late '50's vintage (or fuchsia, that color marking its owner with the status of a "certain occupation") with its extraordinary length, fronted by large breast-like phallic bullets called bumper guards, and ended with an extended rear bumper and the continental wheel, was the status ideal of the low-income strata of Black Americans. A couple of radio antennae in the front and a television antenna on the rear deck lid capped off the exterior look. In the rear passenger area a bar on a cabinet of liquor would be cool. If one couldn't afford this, as most couldn't, the Buick Electra "deuce and a quarter" was popular. This automotive image is the stereotypic ideal rather than the reality since few actually possessed them. But this form of conspicuous consumption, of course, was å mark of status in a society that was rather niggardly about conferring status and access to resources to Black Americans. In this era and socioeconomic stratum the flamboyant automobile marked the extent of achievement a man had attained. But, this form of extravagance was often lamented by their women who would have preferred their men to have invested their wealth in more quiet pursuits such as the support of their children. But, the need for status and the feeling of self-worth had an urgency and a priority that superceded the masculine orientation to the more difficult and demanding attention to family needs. Material (especially manufactured) identity markers of cultural significance appear to be of greater concern to the men of the Black community, although the data from the literature are by no means clear. Women appear to have somewhat less pressing concerns for material identity markers, although they are very much concerned with their physical appearance and so, like most

59

women of the world, do attend to the nature and quality of their cosmetics and dress. Depending upon place and time Black women who are status-conscious will purchase certain identity markers such as designer handbags, designer clothing, and expensive shoes and wear their nails long and painted to complement their attire. But, even when it is within the means of women to purchase high status material goods, their priority orientations are more directed to human relationships the most important of which are family-based networks and the church.

10. History. My anthropological orientation to Black history is not so much a chronicle of names, dates, places, and events, but rather, a temporal ordering of patterns and experience and the diachronically occurring forces that shaped Black culture into what it is today. This perspective has both an objective and a subjective focus. The objective focus examines the external circumstances and temporal order of events that make up particular phases in the historical process. The subjective focus is the chronicle of personal experience by those individuals who are involved in the historical process. To obtain this one must speak to and know the actors whose experience only they can communicate. From the point of view of these people whose experience is the consequence of Black history, and who will be the main players in the development of a future history, we are concerned with understanding their traditions of meaning and experience at both the conscious and unconscious levels as well as at the cognitive, emotional, and pragmatic levels of experience.

Two schools of thought dominate the study of Black history. The Africanist school of thought places emphasis on carryovers of custom and certain forms of social relationship from the Old World to the New World. Melville Herskovits (1941) has been the dominant proponent of this framework. Comparing West African culture with West Indian culture he noted a high degree of similarity of song, poetry, and legend, and a matrifocal emphasis on the importance of mother and children and a relatively weak relationship between husband and wife, with the woman's primary orientation being toward her own natal extended family. The thesis of Herskovits, then, is to explain many New World patterns in terms of the carryovers from the homelands of West Africa.

A dominant opposing school can be found in the works of E.Franklin Frazier (1939, 1949). This can be considered the Slavery school of thought. The thesis of this conceptual framework is that the institution of slavery, as it was practiced in the New World, obliterated the customs and institutions of African origin, especially those dealing with marriage. The horror of the transatlantic voyage, the splitting up of people from their tribal and family members, the regrouping of African slaves with those who spoke different tribal languages and who had practiced different tribal customs, were sufficient conditions to argue that the history and identity of Black Americans are rooted in the tribulations and adaptations of American slavery. The anthropologist sees merit in both these arguments and proceeds by looking for those customs that carry important meanings forward from one generation to the next.

The following are a few of the more powerful symbols of the Black historical experience: a) Africa, the homeland; b) slavery and the obliteration of native culture and social organization; c) emancipation and the awesome challenges of building a Black community; d) racism and poverty; e) separatist religious movements; and f) the civil rights and Black power movements, the latter three of which carry the historical aspects of Black culture into the present. Black history presents a picture of cycles of freedom and oppression; a dialectic moved by migration and struggle, ethnicity and assimilation, and enlivened by a certain transcendental attitude, expressed differently in women and men, but centered in the fundamentalist tradition of Black religion.

11. The culture of poverty. This concept was conceived by the anthropologist Oscar Lewis (1959) in his studies of families living in poverty over long periods of time. Lewis theorized that conditions of poverty had associated with it many economic, social, and psychological features that become built into the culture, the lifestyle, and values of the people. In a sense, the

poverty way of life becomes internalized and self-perpetuating, thereby committing the people to that way of life and precluding any path out of it.

The economic characteristics of poverty include such things as low income and unemployment, unskilled labor, customary pawning, little or no savings, and the pursuit of illegitimate means of acquiring income. The social characteristics of poverty include densely populated neighborhoods, the mother-centered, matrifocal household, crowded living space, little or no privacy, early and promiscuous sexual experience, unstable marriages, alcoholism and physical violence. The psychological characteristics of the culture of poverty include impulsiveness and only short-term future-orientation, inclinations toward sensuality and potentially dangerous excitement, an aggressive disposition, and a tendency to favor gregarious associations with members of the same-sex. The list continues with an authoritarian orientation in status relationships and yet a distrust of political and government authority figures; feelings of insecurity, even desperation, occupying a marginal status; and a fatalistic world view. Lewis believed that because these characteristics were so ingrained and had become foci of values and orientations, it would be more difficult to change this lifestyle than to ameliorate the economic situation of poverty itself.

Critics of this theory offer alternative interpretations of the empirical data (Valentine, 1968; Parker and Kleiner, 1972; Stack, 1975; Eames and Goode, 1977). One thoughtful criticism is that the realities of everyday life permit few, if any, alternatives of behavior, thought, and feeling; that poverty is a grinding tedium from which it is difficult to escape. Another point, which is being supported by a growing body of evidence cited in the above four sources, is that those people who exist in the culture of poverty possess two sets of values and dispositions that reflect a) the poverty of the ghetto and b) the mainstream values that could be expressed should the opportunities become available. Another criticism is that the culture of poverty concept emphasizes the social disorganization and pathological aspects of life and place little emphasis on the creative adaptations to poverty. Stack (1975) has made an earnest and effective attempt to reestablish the balance. Further, Lewis and his proponents have overgeneralized the concept from Puerto Rican and Mexican communities to other areas and cultures of the world where the record demonstrates some refutation of the culture of poverty concept (Mangin, 1970; Leeds, 1971; Safa, 1968). The empirical record on Black American culture reviewed in this book will also contribute to the argument that the culture of poverty is unstable and, given the proper conditions, is eradicable.

V

RELIGION

In the same way that I distinguish between culture as a system of values, codes, and orientations toward the world, and social organization as relational systems of behavior and networks of communication, I will distinguish here between religion and the church. By the church I refer to a) the physical edifice, b) the geographic place in which religious activity takes place and c) the social organization of the church congregation, including all those formal and informal social roles, offices, and activities that are associated with the church. Religion is, analytically speaking, within the cultural realm of the human experience. In fact, it is a strong notion of many anthropologists that religion just may have been the nucleus out of which and the nexus around which human culture became elaborated, for in the very traditional cultures of today, among peoples practicing 2-, 5-, and 10,000 year old traditions, we see religion being the focal point, the ultimate reference, for the other cultural institutions as well as in daily life.

Relatively recently, on the evolutionary time-scale, about the last 200 years, religion has gone through some rather radical changes in certain sectors of human society, viz., the urban, industrialized, westernized sectors. This change was from a primarily nonrational, emotionally based, symbolically expressive religion to a fairly rationalized and somewhat secularized and urbane form of religion. The first form of religion I shall call fundamental, at the risk of having this concept confused with "fundamentalist" religion. Many scholars, including anthropologists, call this form of religion "folk" religion which is commonly practiced by often illiterate or semi-literate peasant farmers around the world. The second form of religion I shall call rationalized religion. It is that religion which is most familiar to the middle classes of Europe and America; religion that appeals more to the rational and intellectual self and to the historical perspective of religion and ethnicity and much less to the emotional self.

65

It is my opinion that the former type is the religion with the real power, the power to facilitate what it was originally intended to accomplish, viz., a group of functions that will be discussed below. Contrary to popular opinion, I believe the latter form of religion has lost its true or original powers by becoming subordinated to human reason, which in this context, has been over-rated with regard to what people assume their religion can accomplish. It is my thesis that the religion of Black culture has maintained many fundamental forms and functions which have endowed its people with a certain moral force needed to withstand the racial domination in the New World. If I were to concede to the Africanist's argument that a good deal of Black culture has carried over from Africa, I would concede that certain aspects of Black religion have their roots in African traditions; in modalities of <u>emotional communication</u>, such as myth, rhythm, and song, that could survive the ordeals of the transatlantic crossing and the institution of slavery.

A Definition of Religion

At this juncture, let me offer a definition of religion which will clarify my perspective on human religion in general and Black religion in particular. It is a definition that has been influenced by other scholars on religion such as Sapir (1949), Geertz (1966), and Spiro (1966), influenced by my work in Africa, and also influenced by my own experience of Black religion in America. My definition is as follows:

Religion derives from the haunting realization of ultimate powerlessness in an inscrutable world, where each person harbors the unquestioning and irrational conviction of the possibility of gaining mystic security by somehow identifying one's self with what can never be known.

It is a "never-ceasing attempt to discover a road to spiritual serenity across the perplexities and dangers of daily life" (Sapir, p. 122), manifesting itself as a system of symbols which acts as the vehicle for establishing powerful moods and motivations through a) the formulation of conceptions of a general order, and through b) rituals to act them out (Geertz, 1966).

66

The components of the <u>religious experience</u> include a configuration of emotional states: Fear, awe, hope, love, the plea, and belief or faith, and sometimes, ecstasy; emotional states that are brought within the context of ultimate values and transcendent truths which generate commitments to certain types of social action oriented to penultimate concerns, the most ultimate of which is the realization of the inevitability of death.

The Components of Religion

There are several components that make up the institution of religion that are necessary for aggregating people into a religious community and fostering a religious sentiment. Here I recognize eight important components of religion in general and Black religion in particular.

1. <u>Ideology</u>. Ideology can be conceived as a system of ideas functioning as a program for thought and action. It must be taught or learned through some process of education and exists on the rational plane of consciousness. The predominant system of ideas is known as the theology. Although drawing from the same body of texts and scripture as other Christian sects Black religion emphasizes and stylizes much differently than the white counterparts. History and daily life shape a person's expression of religion. J. Deotis Roberts (1971) points out that Black religion does a considerable amount of harkening back to the Old Testament:

> Against the consciousness of unjust treatment, an unloving relationship based on racism, and the painful awareness of an unmerciful society, there is a need to believe that God is just, loving, and merciful. This is the reason I believe, why the Old Testament prophets have had a special place in the hearts of black men. Amos' message of social justice sent from a God of justice, Isaiah's condemnation of the feast days of those whose hands are full of blood, and Micah's list of divine requirements--do justly, love mercy, and walk humbly with God--have spoken to the heart of the Negro. Then,

Jesus, who came not to destroy the law and the prophets
but to fulfill the promise by his life, his teachings, and
his cross, demonstrates the very life of this God (p. 71).

It should also be noted here that Black theology is not really
prescribed as it is set down in the Bible, New Testament or Old
Testament. Henry Mitchell (1970), a veteran Black preacher in
his own right, points out that the Black preacher is more likely
to think of the Bible as an inexhaustible source of good
preaching material than as an inert doctrinal and ethical
authority. Rather, he sees it as a body of literature full of
insights--warm and wise and relevant to the everyday problems of
the Black people (p. 113).

But many other aspects of the cultural ideology are also
brought into play within the context of religion, such as political
and economic ideas, and the philosophical/ethical ideas of the
greater civilization of which a particular ethnic group is a part.
The pastors and ministers of Black religion predominantly preach
fundamentalist Christianity and interpret the biblical texts into
rather clear cut ideological programs for thought and action.

2. Moral values. Moral values are prescriptive. They
prescribe patterns of relationship that promise to ensure the
social health and development of the group. They consist of
codes of "shoulds" and "should nots" and often have attendant
rewards and punishments attached to them. Black religion in
particular puts a great emphasis on the familistic values not only
with regard to the family but with regard to the congregation
and the Black people of the world, which is seen as a larger
extension of the family.

3. Mythology. A mythological system consists of symbolic
texts, stories and parables, that offer a surface meaning, which
does not appear real or historically real (such as talking animals),
and a deep symbolic meaning, which proclaims certain truths and
moral principles that are on the nonrational plane and speak an
emotional language, not a rational language. (The term "myth" is
widely misused, referring to a fiction or falsehood or untrue

68

belief or assumption. The term "fallacy" is the more appropriate term to use. The term "myth" should be reserved for the conceptualization I give it here.) Black religion is rich in mythology, being expressed in both the religious and secular contexts. I believe the wealth of mythology is due to the largely emotional nature of Black religion, and the syntax of mythology, the rules and principles for putting ideas together, possibly the legacy of the Old World.

4. <u>Recognition of superhuman beings</u>. This is one aspect of Black religion that probably need not be mentioned because it is a foregone conclusion. However, the interpretation and beliefs about the actions of superhuman beings do vary from sect to sect, and although fundamentalist Christianity prescribes a relative uniformity about the nature, number, and existence of these beings, the particular emphasis placed on these beings during a church service does vary. One important emphasis in many churches is the holy ghost or holy spirit which may enter the body of the worshipper in a trance state and enable that person to speak in tongues.

5. <u>Charismatic leadership</u>. This is a very important element in Black religion. Religious leaders are symbols of the ideals and mission of the religious congregation. He or she is looked upon as the moral force of and the example for the congregation. The church service, or the church itself, may succeed or fail depending on those qualities of the religious leader. As W.E.B. DuBois writes, in his <u>The Souls of Blackfolk</u> (pp. 190-1):

> The preacher is the most unique personality developed by the Negro on American soil. A leader, a politician, an orator, a 'boss,' an intriguer, an idealist--all these he is, and ever, too, the center of a group of men, now twenty, now a thousand in number. The combination of a certain adroitness with deep-seated earnestness, of tack with consummate ability, gave him his preeminence, and helps him maintain it (quoted in Mays and Nicholson, p. 38).

The religious leader requires a certain strength of personality, a power to communicate, an ability to bring the members together into a spiritual unity that will further the needs of the individual as well as the group. Charisma lubricates the channels of communication and quickens the members' coming together as a spiritual community into a commonly shared religious experience.

Some of the qualities and requirements of a religious leader, noted in Williams' study of an urban fundamentalist Protestant sect (1974), can be generalized to many Black churches. The religious leader must be able to generate excitement through his or her delivery of biblical text and through the articulation of the religious aspirations of the congregation. The religious leader must maintain an air of distinctiveness, if not aloofness, with material possessions, wealth, and education while at the same time assuring the congregation of his or her empathy with them. The religious leader must be an entertainer and be able to inject fun into the service with humor within the bounds of recognized propriety. He or she must be able to attract new members and hold the present members. And, more appropriate for males, the religious leader must conduct his personal life in such a manner that he functions as a role model for his congregation and frustrates the possibilities for gossip and scandal (Ibid., pp.49-50).

Joseph Washington makes a more emphatic statement about the significance of the Black preacher. He casts him into the role of a culture hero:

> ...when the black preacher is really a turned-on man he
> still is to be reckoned with as a culture hero of the
> black folk. The key to the black culture hero is that he
> be able to entertain, be clever, and possess the capacity
> to be economically well off without having to grind it
> out for a living. The preacher is rivaled today by the
> hustler, the comedian, the athlete, the singer, and the
> musician as the culture hero of the black folk. But the
> point is that the black folk look to these black ritualists
> as heroes, and, the hero is always the much berated

black male, not the black woman. The black preacher
may be losing ground, but he is still a potent hero
among black women, who, after all, are the supporters of
the congregation (p. 32).

There are relatively few ministers who are academically
trained. Many are simply inspired to the calling and develop
their own skills and then test the waters to see if they can
attract a congregation. In their two year study, Mays and
Nicholson learned that academic training is not a necessary
requirement and is really not a measure of a preacher's skills
(Ibid. p. 40). Nevertheless, education of the clergy is steadily
growing as ministers grapple with questions and problems that
range beyond the boundaries of their own religious community.

6. Music. Music plays a major role in carrying on the
service. Gospel music is widely recognized as the distinctive
feature of Black religion in America. This recognition ranges far
beyond the ethnic boundaries of Black people and national
boundaries of the United States as the international sales of
gospel music albums attest. Gospel music, as with other genre of
Black music, such as the blues, is the emotional memory of the
Black experience. And, it is more. Black music is
improvisational, which allows the creativity of Black culture to
come through. Black music is driven by antiphonal singing and
polymetrical rhythm, with the music being played in 4/4 meter
while the congregation snaps their fingers, claps their hands and
stamps their feet in 2/4 meter. The gradual build-up of musical
tension to an emotional climax, renders gospel music an important
vehicle for attaining the heights of religious emotional
experience.

7. Ritual. Ritual is the symbolic language of behavior. We
can define ritual as a prescription or formula for minutely
defined behavior which is often highly stylized and performed the
same way each time the ritual is called for. This behavior may
be verbal or nonverbal and fall into one or more of the following
general categories: It may be exhortative whereby a plea in
made to the spirits or God to incite the beings of beyond into

some form of laudable or good actions. The ritual may be
sacrificial whereby a person or group makes a sacrifice to help
right a wrong or to encourage the superhuman beings to use
their powers to assist the person or group. Or, the ritual may
be a rite of passage whereby a person or group makes a
transition from one state of existence to another. Rites of
passage include ceremonies of birth, confirmation, puberty,
marriage, and death, and also, the transition from an everyday
secular state of mind to a religious state of mind, often in an
altered state of consciousness. The rituals of Black religion
include sacrifice, confession and testimonial, gospel music and
prayer, healing, and the ritual delivery of the preacher. Joseph
Washington, writing with the sensitivity of a cultural
anthropologist, expresses how Black religion is driven by its
ritual:

> The religion of black folk is a religion of ritual, drama,
> and 'dialectical catharsis.' The key to black folk religion
> is the power with which the black unconscious is stirred
> through ritualization. This religion of ritual power is
> not limited to churches or the sacred; it is best
> perceived as a real blend of the sacred and secular--
> that's where black religion is, for that is where life is.
> Those who possess this ritual power are black
> preachers, disk jockeys, singers, musicians, hustlers,
> comedians, and athletes. These ritualists are in the
> long line of black ritualists, they have 'soul power'
> because they have tapped the 'soul tradition' at its
> African roots (p. 32).

8. Ecstasy. The ecstatic state is the final element of Black
religion to note here. It refers to the heights of religious
experience realized in an altered state of consciousness, or trance
state, and often results in the speaking in tongues, frenzied
movements, crying for joy, and a belief that the holy spirit has
entered the body confirming one's unity with the Godhead. The
state of disinhibition that worshipers come to the service with,
this readiness for "letting go," accelerates the worshipers into a

72

religious state of mind. This religious state of mind is in the realm of the spiritual.

The all-consuming passionate abandon so characteristic of Black culture worship has no doubt been an escape from brutal reality and a survival technique. But in a more positive sense of this abandon, the freedom has been the evidence that spirit supersedes environment--that life at the spiritual level is real and abundant no matter what (Washington, 1971, p. 34).

The Functions of Religion
Religion has both a structure and a function. What I have here identified as the components of religion in Black culture refer, at least in part, to the structural elements. But just as important to a cultural institution is its function. Although there are several definitions of the term function, here I refer to two types. The first type of function deals with the satisfaction of human needs. Human beings are rather pragmatic animals and if certain behaviors and customs work for us we keep it, and if it doesn't, we cast it aside. The second type of function refers to those actions, behavior patterns, customs, or attitudes and values that are a consequence of some set of prior conditions. That is, an aspect of society, culture, or behavior which is in a cause-effect relationship with other aspects of its environment. Thus, the functions of Black religion are responses to human needs, to Black history, to the existential conditions of American society, and to the ideals, values, and cultural goals of Black people.

The functions of religion can be subsumed under the five major functions of culture (chapter III), viz., adaptation, explanation, remembrance, expression, and utility. For our purposes here I identify ten major functions of Black religion, functions that serve the personal and group needs of the congregation and often reach beyond the congregation to serving the needs of the wider community. These functions have their origins both in the deep traditional past of humanity and, more particularly, are functions that were and still are highly valued in the traditions of the rural South. You may notice that the first

73

two functions comprise something of an "environment" for the operation of functions 3-9, which can be conceived as stages of the religious process. Each stage creates its own "environment" for the development of the next stage. And so a religious experiential process is built up, where each participating member makes unconscious choices about how far along this process one will go.

1. Refuge. The church is a sanctuary. Its space is sacrosanct. It is a sanctum from the rest of the world. The congregation owns the church. They possess it and claim dominion over it. They act as a corporation with an identity separate from their personal identity and come together to conduct the business of spiritual endeavor. The church is a special place that directs one's orientation away from the petty issues of the mundane life. It is a place to feel secure within a large group, to experience joy with one's intimates, and to reaffirm a moral attitude. Many Black religious sects do not just hold service on Saturday or Sunday morning, but several times a week, and for several hours at a time. This expresses the importance these people place on the role of religion in everyday life.

2. A warm climate of social acceptance. A necessary condition for building a strong feeling of togetherness and the sense of sharing a common experience is the trust of each other and the belief, if not the knowledge, that each participating member is committed to the support of the others. A warm climate of social acceptance precludes judgments against anyone in the congregation. Rather, if there are infractions of the religious or social norms by a member, the congregation or its spokesman may offer redemption in exchange for reparations and compliance. There will be the promise of forgiveness as an answer to one's remorse. But, ostracism is also an alternative where no offer to change bad behavior is shown by an offending party. This social climate follows the model of familistic values where the members of the congregation view each other as brothers and sisters in a wider religious family or familistic community.

3. Active participation of all members. It is implicitly understood by the members of the congregation, and often explicitly urged by the preacher, that all present take an active part in carrying the service. Active participation of all insures the total involvement of the individual. Those who choose to merely "observe" and remain apart from the actively involved members may drive a wedge into the continuity and flow of the service and make others feel self-conscious or more reserved in their participation.

Active participation of all insures the effectiveness of what anthropologists call rites of intensification, rites that reinforce the ideals, values, and goals of the group and reaffirm the validity of the pursuits of the members. This intensification and reaffirmation occurs both at the social level in maintaining bonds of social solidarity and at the emotional level in maintaining a certain strength of motivation and direction in social and religious endeavors.

4. Confession. Since no one is perfect, we are bound to commit infractions against the moral codes we live by; or, in the idiom of religion, we are bound to sin. Although manifesting itself differently in the Catholic ritual as compared with the Protestant sects, and even seeing minor variations of its expression among these sects, confession remains one of those universals of religious expression. Confession is a very efficient modality for the expiation of guilt. For most people, guilt is a very uncomfortable feeling; for some it is rather intolerable. Therefore, people need to find ways of relieving themselves of the discomfort of guilt because it is one cause of stress. Therefore, the path toward the alleviation of the discomfort of guilt and accompanying stress is to confess. This confession becomes the precondition for the congregation's forgiveness which will be the cure for that affliction. Confession is most often a precondition for the acts of repentance and redemption which follow.

5. <u>Repentance</u>. Repentance is the desire to amend one's sinful acts. It is one stage in the process of negating the ostracism of the religious community and becoming reunited with that community. So long as one finds meaning in the actions of the religious community there will be motivation to reconcile one's self to that community. Those who have no such need and who are predisposed to infraction of moral norms usually remain outside the religious community and psychologically alien to it. Through repentance one makes one's case for redemption.

6. <u>Sacrifice</u>. An exchange relationship with God is often manifested in the form of sacrifice. The act of sacrifice is a symbolic vehicle for accomplishing such tasks as repentance and redemption in the stages of the religious enterprise. The sacrificial act may not always be recognized as such because of the common belief that sacrifice is the offering of a slain animal or some such thing. But, sacrifice may also be conceived as the act of giving up something of value for the sake of something of greater value. For example, when someone who has little money offers a large sum of money in order to achieve a sense of moral worth--material offering for spiritual status, this offering of something dear is a sacrifice. One who has fallen out of favor with the group or who has experienced this falling out with God has a need to be reintegrated; has the need to give up something of value in order to nullify the disinheritance and reestablish communion. Sacrifice is the gesture signifying a meaningful intention in that regard.

7. <u>Redemption</u>. To buy one's self back into favor, the favor of Christ, the favor of the church congregation, is redemption. This must be done in a number of ways: One can make a monetary offering to the church, which is a form of sacrifice. One may offer service to the church or to the community. One may offer a public testimonial to the congregation as to the nature of one's impropriety or sin and a promise to make up for any wrongs done to others. One may offer prayer as a plea and as a promise and in recognition of Christ. The experience of the expiation of the burdens of sin will facilitate a feeling of belonging to the religious community and to the family of God.

8. <u>Catharsis</u>. The discharging of tension and the relief that is experienced as a consequence is one of the more "gutsy" and pragmatic functions of religion. This tension is both physical, muscular, and emotional. It is a very important part of the religious service because people bring to the church all the stresses caused by the problems and frustrations of daily life; and within the context of the church, people find a modality for alleviating these stresses. And, further, total participation and total involvement generate a common experience which, by the very nature of that assumption of a common experience shared by all, diffuses that tension, breaks down the level of stress, through that symbolic communication process of prayer, music, and joyful togetherness. The high-point of catharsis is that emotional culmination achieved in the ecstatic experience.

Shouting is a rather distinctive feature of the Black service that signifies the emotional meaning of worship. According to Washington (1971) there are many Black worshipers who would consider the service a failure if there were no shouting. "The measure of Black authenticity...would have to be not how much shouting is done, but out of what wellsprings of spiritual motivation it comes" (p. 44). Shouting and answering the preacher's pronouncements expresses the personal religious experience of the worshiper. And this becomes a mode of catharsis. Washington appreciates this when he states that:

> There is also the seldom articulated awareness that shouting is healing and cathartic, not only expressing joy at the presence of God, but also healthily purging guilt, sorrow, pain, and frustration (Ibid., pp. 45-6).

9. <u>Healing</u>. A great many physical ailments and emotional disorders are caused by stress. Contrary to popular opinion, stress-related illnesses are not unique to modern, rapid-paced, industrialized society. These kinds of illnesses are ancient. That is why I believe that the "oldest profession in the world" is not

what most people think of, but rather, the oldest profession is shamanism, that craft practiced by the medicine man. Through a thousand generations human beings worldwide have evolved shamanism within the institution of religion to serve human ills. It is the profession most closely related to the psychiatrist, for the shaman knows what medicines are found in nature, mainly in plants, but he or she also knows what kinds of emotional communication is needed to alleviate the symptoms.

This emotional communication is facilitated not only between doctor and patient, but also, the shaman directs communication between the patient and his or her primary group. A good religious leader will be skillful in manipulating a mood in his congregation and bringing this mood to a climax, that, on a physiological level, stimulates the brain to release the endorphins responsible for the high energy, elevated mood, obliteration of pain, and stress reduction. On the social level this shamanistic religious leader will reaffirm his or her authority by the extraordinary powers demonstrated and intensify the bonds of the group. Only a few members need experience a healing for the leader and the congregation to reaffirm their institution. One reason for identifying Black religion as fundamental is because of this very ancient and effective component of the religious service and the religious experience.

10. Crisis Intervention. A final psychosocial function of Black religion, shared by many religions around the world, is the ability and willingness of designated members to intervene in or take part in a crisis of a fellow member or family. The term crisis refers to an important change in a person's or family's life and the necessity to reestablish a steady state after a significant discontinuity or disruption occurs. The most common crises are marriage and death, and these are handled in a highly structured manner centered around the marriage and funeral ceremonies, respectively. The more common notion of crisis refers to the more acute and painful types of unpredictable occurrences. These crises that the church members become involved in, employing the resources of their religion, include serious illness, family

violence, marital discord, adolescent rebellion, economic misfortune, and natural disaster.

These, then, are ten important functions of Black religion. As noted earlier, types 1 and 2 of our functional list make up the environment needed to carry on the other functions. Types 3 through 9 make up the developmental psychosocial experience of the religious process. And, type 10 is the crisis mechanism, called upon to deal with both a) the planned and predictable emerging situations and b) the acute and unpredictable situations that emerge suddenly and without warning.

In conclusion, the structure and the functions of Black religion are very much tied into Black culture as a whole. It is common knowledge among people themselves, and, on occasion the Black intellectual writes about it. Joseph Washington sees Black religion as the core of Black culture because Black religion is an experiential religion, expressing the common every day problems and experience of Black people. As Washington puts it:

> Black culture has its special domain in black folk religion, the locus where black people have proved and preserved their identity. Black folk religion is experiential first and foremost. It begins and ends in the experience of the black folk. It is a religion of acting out or dramatizing the experience of the people through uninhibited feeling expressed in powerful tones (p. 31).

VI

A TYPOLOGY OF BLACK DOMESTIC SOCIAL ORGANIZATION

The organization of the family is influenced by many different forces operating in the wider society. Our concept of the family must not be considered in some absolute sense such as the "right" kind of family, the way God intended the family to be, or some cultural stereotype of the "Family" which assumes only one legitimate form. The danger here is that should one assume a family structure in absolute terms, other forms of family organization might then be considered "abnormal," "disorganized," "pathological," "deviant," or "broken," thereby passing ethnocentric judgement upon other family forms as illegitimate. Rather, we must employ a perspective of cultural relativity and see the organization of the family as adaptive; an adaptation to the physical, social, cultural, political, and economic forces that differentially impinge upon members of the various ethnic groups of a population.

My thesis here is that the Black family cannot be conceived or evaluated solely in terms of the American cultural ideal, but rather, must be understood as a very flexible array of sets of relationships, often based on very pragmatic principles that maximize the benefits of both the individual and that group to which the individual belongs. There is, in fact, an extensive range of forms of relationship that Black Americans participate in. These forms are not exclusive to Black Americans but are realms of social life that are practiced by human beings around the world. What uniqueness or distinctiveness an ethnic group manifests is due to a) the modal emphasis placed on one or more forms of relationship, b) the principles in terms of which the members of the domestic group carry on their respective roles, and c) the style in which it is played out.

The Pair Bond
The most fundamental unit of human relationship is the pair-bond. It is the basis for forging those ramifying relationships of which the various types of groups and networks are made up.

The mother-child bond. The most fundamental of all human ties, and that which has the most profound impact on the

81

```
 o-----------------o-----------------o-------------o----
Pair-Bond          Peer Group        Nuclear       Matri-
a. mo-child        a. male           Family        focal
b. fa.-child       b. female         a. original   Unit
c. consort         c. child          b. blended
d. male            d. adolesc.
e. female          e. adult
```

developing personality, is the mother-child bond. Becoming
pregnant and bearing a child is, in Black culture, natural and
self-validating, regardless of the marital status of the girl or
woman having that child. The bond between mother and child is
intense and is reinforced by the wider kin-group. But unless the
woman is in a secure marriage and/or has the firm support of
her kin group, her role of mother will be difficult. If a young
Black woman is not married and is immature, say, an adolescent,
and cannot take the major responsibility for caring for her child,
another member of the kin group may assume that childrearing
role for a time, thereby entitling that surrogate parent to full
parental rights over that child. As Aschenbrenner and Stack
both attest to in their ethnographies, "mama" is that person who
raised that child up; the sociological mother is given the greater
recognition, as opposed to the biological mother who did not rear
the child. In Stack's study, 80% of the recognized mothers were
the natural mothers of their children (p.49).

   The father-child bond. The father-child bond is certainly a
more tenuous relationship when the economic conditions of the
Black community impose serious constraints on that father's
ability to support that mother and her child. Given the economic
principles of American society and the definition of the male role
in the modern urban environment, the ability of a man to fulfill
his role as father is very closely tied to his ability to access
resources in a stable or regular manner over a long period of
time. Therefore, the genitor, or biological

A Typology of Black Domestic Social Organization

```
---o----------------o----------------o----------o
```

| Andro-
centric
Domestic
Network | Extended
Family
(bilateral,
multi-
generational,
consanguineal,
affinal,
fictive) | Community
(often
defined
by church) | Ethnic
Group |

father, has a range of options and constrictions in assuming his father role to his child. He may choose not to recognize the child as his, which is more common among young unemployed teenagers. He may maintain only sporadic relations with the mother of his child and therefore assume his role to his child only occasionally. Or, he may be relatively economically secure and carry on a long term consensual or marital relationship with the mother of his child and hence be a consistent father to his child. The relative economic security of a man usually refers to more than his job. It also commonly involves his own extended kin from whom he accesses material and emotional resources and to whom he reciprocally offers a share of his own resources. A Black father's parental rights, then, is validated relative to his and his family's ability to support that child (Stack, p. 51).

One area of father-child relations that is hardly elaborated in the social science literature, but has greater expression in film, poetry, and fiction, is the symbolism, the emotional meaning, a child has for its father. In the film "Nothing But A Man" (1966) the central male character is the nexus of his father and his child. Duff seeks out his father whom he finds hostile and rejecting. Duff's father, burdened by the guilt of not being able to care for his son through Duff's childhood, pained by the sorrow of not being able to fulfill his own need to love and father his son, has taken to alcohol in order to anesthetize his sense of failure as a father and as a burden to the woman who supports him. Duff, nevertheless, tries to reestablish a relationship with his father, but the father dies in Duff's arms

83

from the complications of alcoholism and depression. Duff himself has had a child which lives with a woman caretaker, the mother having abandoned the child. Duff, being in a new marriage, does not recognize his son because he fears that this child will interfere with his relationship with his new wife. But, upon her insistence, he reluctantly brings his son into his new marriage after the death of his father, determined to do a better job of fathering than his own father had done.

Duff's relationship with his own father and with his son is rather archetypal for fathers living in the context of scarce resources. The barriers to the fulfillment of this very basic element of masculine identity creates a great deal of ambivalence in a man. The child symbolically represents a challenge to a man who responds often with deeply charged emotions. A child, especially a son, may remind a man of his own childhood and of his difficulties with his own father. The challenge here may be for a man to relate to his son differently from the way his father treated him. On the other hand his son offers the challenge to fulfill the needs of, not one, but two masculine identities: The child needs his father to identify with in an enduring long-term relationship and the father needs to fulfill his own masculine role requirements by being responsible for his child and exercising a certain parental power over his child that results in the development of a strong and viable human being capable of giving the father a deserved respect and promise of support in the father's elderhood.

The consort pair. Another important, if not critical, bond is what I will call here the consort pair. By this term I refer to any adult heterosexual relationship maintained through mutual sexual and economic pursuits. It may exist in the form of a legal marriage, a consensual union, or a short-term casual relationship. A consort pair may be a very difficult if not unstable relationship. If the economic and social pressures among friends are great, they are even greater on a heterosexual relationship. The competition among men for the attentions of a particular women and the evaluations of women regarding the advantages or difficulties she may be entering into with a particular man, and the demands that can be imposed upon one-another render the consort relationship fraught with ambivalence, and yet often highly charged with romance and sexual promise.

The male-male bond. To carry out the logic of the primary pair-bond categories we note the male bond to other males, usually oriented to business, economic, political, and friendship goals.

The female-female bond. The relationship of a female to other females is normally oriented to economic, friendship, and social pursuits. These relationships are normally more centered in the domestic network, more child-oriented, and involved in the maintenance of the network of reciprocity that distributes valuable resources among its members (Stack, 1974). These latter two categories of relationship, shall come under discussion in the context of the more complex domestic institutions taken up later.

The Peer Group

The peer group is another universal group structure that has a great deal of importance during the childhood socialization period. However, the peer group can take several different forms as shown in our schematic. On a world-wide scale the peer group is normally a same-sex group. And, for logical purposes we can categorize the various peer group forms by age and sex. So, we get a) male peer groups and b) female peer groups, c) peer groups of young children (who are gaining facility with language and communication), d) adolescents (psychologically the most important form), and e) adults.

Depending upon the stage of development a child is in and the type of society the peer group exists in, it may be mixed or same-sex. Normally, toddlers through children of age 6 or 7 mix sexes freely. After ages eight or nine, during the latency stage of development, boys and girls normally voluntarily segregate themselves and continue to reinforce each other's social and sexual identity and sex role as their culture defines it. In traditional societies adolescents are normally segregated by their respective families until marriage arrangements are carried out.

85

In modern urban societies, reinforced by the public school system, the sexes are allowed to mix, at least socially. In the adolescent phase of peer group organization we find an intensification of activities that contribute to the definition of the sex role. This is the phase where special interest group involvement becomes more intense, with an emphasis on same-sex activities, such as school sports. In the context of economic and cultural deprivation, we find the greatest probability of the formation of boys gangs.

The Nuclear Family

The next social structure to consider is the nuclear family. This institution is found universally among the human populations of the world. It is a normal inclination for a man and a woman who come together for sexual and economic pursuits, and who issue forth offspring, to form a more or less enduring bond. This family unit consists of eight social roles: husband/father, wife/mother, son/brother, and daughter/sister (the exception being the single-child family). The actual behaviors and tasks prescribed by the culture to be carried out by the individuals occupying those roles differs to some extent from society to society. These roles are critical for the normal functioning and development of the family.

One complication of nuclear family dynamics that is much too seldom discussed in the literature is the consequence of divorce and remarriage which brings about the phenomenon of the blended family, more commonly recognized as step-parents and step-children. This adds to the complexity of the standard eight role model usually acknowledged in the sociological literature. Although blended families face considerable problems of adaptation in the general population, within the Black reconstituted nuclear family the issues to be resolved may be even more acute because of the added stresses that Black Americans face in the day-to-day. Therefore, in noting the nuclear family as one such type of domestic group organization we must also recognize two types of nuclear family: the original form, where each parent brings no children from previous relationships into the marriage, and the blended form, where one or both spouses bring children of previous relationships into the new marriage. Regardless of the form of nuclear family arrangement taking place, it is often the case that a Black marriage may be the end result of a long series of negotiations carried out between the marrying pair and between each spouse and their respective families, primarily because of their savvy about the socioeconomic difficulties involved and the importance of that marital relationship (Aschenbrenner, 1975). As will be discussed later, it appears that, because of the Black culturally conditioned attitudes toward children, the acceptance of step-children is considerably easier among Black families than among their white counterparts.

To better understand the dynamics and principles of Black domestic organization from the analytical perspective I wish to introduce a few concepts that might prove useful in understanding ethnographic data on Black families. The structure of the institution of marriage and the nuclear family are made up of the roles that the respective members of the family carry out. Roles have, as their basic elements, configurations of rights and duties. Family rights in particular, and social role rights in general, are of two kinds. First, there are exclusive rights which exclude others from a sphere of social activity. Most notably, monogamy, the marriage of one man to one woman, excludes any other person except the respective spouses from sexual access. In the general context, legitimately acquired money and land are two other commodities to which persons normally maintain exclusive rights. The second order of rights is called complementary rights. These are more complicated in structure. A complementary right must be fulfilled by another person whose duty it is to satisfy one's claim to that right. For example, in many societies it is a husband's duty to acquire food resources, such as crops, or to acquire money in order to buy these food resources. It is the wife's right to have access to these resources in order to be sustained from day to day. And, it is the wife's duty to prepare these food resources as meals for the family to consume; and it is the right of the husband to have his meals prepared for him. In the example of monogamous marriage we can find exclusive and complementary rights combined, since

87

monogamy defines an exclusive sexual relationship, and, as is
very well defined in the more traditional societies, it is a wife's
duty to provide sexual availability to her husband, i.e., it is a
husband's right to have sexual access to his wife. And, it is
usually defined vice versa where a wife has similar rights to her
husband's attentions. These rights and duties are the "building
blocks" of the structure of family organization. They provide
what we can call the infrastructure for all human institutions.
However, the definition and meaning of these various rights and
duties and the prescriptions for how they are carried out differ
from one ethnic group to another, from one culture to another.

The Black nuclear family has tended to be a more tenuous
institution than the nuclear families of white society, at least the
white middle class society. The host of causes for the
difficulties in maintaining nuclear family stability, and
consequently, fostering a matrifocal form of domestic
organization, are considered in the next section. Certainly, it is
not difficult to recognize the economic factors, most particularly
the stresses of poverty and the tenuousness of employment that
work against nuclear family integration. But, less recognized is
the factor of consanguineal loyalties, commitments to one's
blood-relations, most particularly the extended family with whom
one may have long-lasting and relatively intense associations.
This integration into the extended kinship network, then, plays
down the importance of the marital relationship. One is less
dependent upon a spouse for emotional communication when
there is a large body of kin with whom to relate. On the other
hand, Black nuclear families often need the firm support of the
extended kin on both sides of the relationship in order to foster
an enduring nuclear family integration. Otherwise, if the couple
really wish to marry against the sentiments of one or both of the
extended kin, the couple may just have to completely extricate
themselves from their kin relationships, and that requires that
couple to be completely self-sufficient. This form of dependency
upon one's extended kin that is typical in Black society is
something that members of the white middle classes of society
are coming to experience as economic pressures mount, the rate

of divorce increases, and as support from the wider community becomes more and more urgent.

There is a certain tension between spouses and between each spouse and their respective kin among Black Americans; a tension that may be found in other ethnic groups as well, but is rather emphasized in Black domestic organization. This tension was recognized by Elizabeth Bott (1971), a sociologist and psychoanalyst, who has done research in London and the United States. Although originally known as the Bott hypothesis, it appears to be more of a social law. It is conceived as follows: The firmer the loyalties to consanguineal kin the more tenuous the marriage tie. The firmer the marriage tie the looser the commitments are to one's consanguines.

The direction of one's commitments usually hinges upon the economic power of the husband. A man who makes enough money to easily support his family comfortably is self-sufficient, and hence, that family is much less dependent upon others for economic support. And, among the white middle class we do in fact find a considerable nucleation of family life where attachments to extended kin for everyday business and relationships are rather tenuous. However, this nucleation phenomenon is much less in evidence among the Black middle class. Rather, we see a maintenance of extended family relations as well as the nuclear family unit. I believe there are at least two reasons for this. First of all there is a long tradition, a southern rural tradition, of maintaining firm ties to one's extended kin and an appreciation of the enduring support and solidarity that comes with these associations. And second, the racism, discrimination, and oppression that has been a tradition of the white society limits the possibilities of assimilation into the general society by Blacks. This makes the extended kin more significant, more important in terms of mutual support and social enrichment.

The Matrifocal Unit

The fourth form of domestic organization is the matrifocal unit. This may refer to a particular woman and her children occupying a particular house or apartment, the matrifocal household, or it may refer to a wider generality of successive generations of matrifocal-based domestic units carried out as a viable form of adaptation to the conditions of urban poverty. The concept and the reality of matrifocality has been widely recognized by social scientists and social service personnel alike, yet has not always been well understood. Such terms as "the broken family," "the matriarchal family," or "the single parent family," have helped create a misconception about this organizational form along with a great deal of ethnocentric value judgments levelled against it.

The anthropologist sees this as one pattern of adaptation to forces often beyond one's control. It is a household consisting of a woman and her children, but it is not normally considered the family, because those members regarded as family are not defined by who lives in a particular house, but rather by the network of kin ties and mutual support that extend through several, if not many, households. Matrifocality is not a cultural ideal that is strived toward; it is not a habit or a pattern that occurs automatically, so to speak, out of Black cultural traditions, although some writers have attempted to explain matrifocality by going back to African domestic patterns. Rather, this pattern of domestic organization is shaped by social and cultural forces both within Black cultural tradition and outside of it and generates a social pattern of greater complexity than many have recognized.

Here I shall identify eight major variables that act as forces generating the matrifocal household, where a women maintains the authority over and responsibility for her children.

1. Low sex ratio. The first variable is a low sex ratio. This is especially true for those communities recognized as lower class within the economic zone of poverty. There are many more women than there are men. Therefore, men, by their very numbers, are scarce. This is true for two major reasons. First

of all, there is a very high mortality rate among men. High male mortality occurs from a high rate of homicide in ghetto communities where stress and frustration levels are very high, and, with the aid of alcohol and other psychoactive drugs, impulses, especially impulses of rage and aggression have little inhibition. Further, high male mortality is a consequence of drug overdoses, especially since the late '70's and '80's when dangerous drugs have become increasingly available to younger men and children. A second important factor for the low sex ratio is the incarceration of men in state and federal prisons. Where major avenues for legitimate employment are blocked illegitimate paths will be taken; where available jobs pay so little as to be demeaning and insignificant to a man's needs, illegal activities often offer more promise for accessing resources to satisfy those needs.

2. Economic insecurity. The second major variable contributing to the matrifocal household is economic insecurity, i.e., joblessness. Going from one menial job to another does not promise adequate security for a woman and her children with whom a man desires to be a husband and father. And, the illegitimate paths to accessing money and other material resources is tenuous as well and offers no promise of the predictability and security from day to day that a woman needs to create a stable home for her children. Further, the stresses a man undergoes in living out his masculine role creates the probability for him to fall short of the American cultural ideal and creates a wedge that is driven into the possibilities of a marital relationship.

3. A woman's attitude toward marriage. A woman's attitude toward marriage is guarded and considered a high risk enterprise. This is a very realistic appraisal given the precariousness of economic life among a great proportion of Black Americans. Nevertheless, marriage is highly regarded; it is a romantic ideal that is much talked about and made the theme in a great deal of Black music. Yet, a woman is often pressured by her natal kin not to marry because her kin may be deprived of that woman's resources if she does marry, and, a woman must weigh the costs and benefits accruing to the types of commitments she makes.

4. <u>A woman's attitude toward motherhood</u>. Her attitude toward motherhood is a very positive one. Motherhood is highly valued by her and her extended family. It is an elevation of status for a woman to become a mother, regardless of whether she is married or not. The cultural values on children are very positive and the status of womanhood is defined in terms of their presence as her offspring. Black women stand out in contrast to their white counterparts in their responses to the presence of children, any children. Black women light up, become very warm in their contact with children, regardless of whether a child is Black or Caucasian. Black women appear to take a more intense interest in children. The literature on this issue is almost nonexistent, but this writer's impressions about this contrast are strong.

5. <u>A man's attitude toward marriage</u>. Men's attitudes toward marriage, like their female counterparts, are closely tied in with their connections to their consanguineal kin. A man may hesitate to marry because of the obligations they have established with their own kin. Both Stack and Aschenbrenner document the conflicts that are generated when a man considers marrying because those new commitments to his spouse, in that zero-sum game, will mean less resources that he will contribute to his natal kindred.

Informal consensual unions with women, then, have less pressures associated with his relationships with both his mate and his kindred. But, when a man is maintaining consensual relationships with women, his women are similarly open to or are having relationships with other men. Therefore, he must work at his relationships in several ways. If he is genuinely in love with a particular woman he must make sacrifices of time, money, and service, to show her he is worth her time. Regardless of how strongly he feels toward her he usually maintains a posture of dominance, not merely as an act of masculine bravado, but also to control her. As Aschenbrenner has shown, a man attempts to control his woman; for money, for fidelity, for affection. He wants her when he needs her and he doesn't want her giving her resources away to other men. A man's attentions to a woman may also be ingenuine and he may act at loving her in order to exploit her interest in him and win sexual moments and material gains. This type of person is what Aschenbrenner's respondents called the "would-be pimp" (p. 44). But, generally, Black women are savvy and they are very cautious about men and work hard to maintain their sense of independence from men. When they do give in to a man they may very well be doing it with full knowledge of the man's intentions, yet with the resignation that their momentary need for a man's love is worth it.

And it is this dynamic tension between the sexes that helps develop that romantic intensity and motivates men to develop their verbal talents, their "rap," to the level of an art form, for their "talk" is what lubricates their channels of communication and sociality and accesses them into the networks of friends and lovers.

In sum, a variety of forces mitigate against a man's serious consideration of marriage and conditions his attitude against marriage: his loyalty to his personal kindred, his peer group affiliations which would be threatened by a marital commitment, the common ghetto man's attitude toward women as objects of exploitation (highlighted in Hannerz, 1969), high probability of sustenance in the day-to-day through a man's affiliations with a number of women, and, underlying all of this, an environment of poverty, a ghetto milieu, which offers joblessness and menial work and turns a man away from work as a mode of sustenance and toward accessible people for resources in kind.

6. High fertility rate. The relatively high fertility rate among Black women follows from the fourth variable of a woman's attitude toward motherhood. This is an issue that has stirred a great deal of controversy and has been not very well understood by professionals and lay-people alike. Here I will identify twelve factors that contribute to this high fertility rate,

some of which are reflected in the fourth variable on a woman's attitudes toward motherhood.

6.1. The definition of womanhood and the status of adulthood is based on the role of the mother.

6.2. The intrinsic value of children; children valued and loved for their own sake, just because they are, makes them a desirable presence.

6.3. The bearing of a child brings a gain in status for the mother, both because of the meaning of motherhood and that value placed on children.

6.4. Single-parenthood is not a stigma. Women appreciate the risks of marriage, carry on intense romantic affairs with men, yet remain independent of those men.

6.5. A man may coax his woman to have his child. It is part of the masculine identity to sire children and to signify to his peers the presence of those children whether or not he fathers those children, i.e., validates his parental rights to those children.

6.6. The burdens of childcare are diffused through the kin network. Because her family is taking over some of the tasks of the mother she becomes obligated to return certain services to them. This makes a mother's responsibility and commitments not just to her children but to her extended family, her personal kindred, as well. In this sharing of the burdens of the total family, with childcare being just one responsibility in the constellation of duties, a woman's burden of childcare becomes lessened while her responsibilities to her personal kindred become broadened.

6.7. Mothers know they may very likely be able to access the resources of the biological fathers when their needs are pressing while maintaining their independence from these men. As Carol Stack notes in her ethnography, the fathers of a woman's children are often considered as friends of the family in fragile yet continuing relationships over time. Sometimes, when a woman has no particular man she is associating with, she may "choke" one or more of the fathers of her children to satisfy a timely need for economic support (p. 119).

6.8. Peer pressure may encourage a woman to have a child. Especially among young women still in their adolescence who have had one or more children, the friend who is still childless is urged to become like her peers so that she will become like them and thereby win a greater acceptance among them.

6.9. Privacy is often very highly valued. Many women, who live in relatively crowded quarters, as is fairly typical in poverty areas, gain a greater availability of privacy after having a child. Where a woman may have shared a bedroom with a sister or other siblings, once she has a baby she may get a room of her own. This is a luxury for many who live in overcrowded apartments and tenements and who have little access to their own privacy. Also, a woman who bears her first child avails herself of the right of public assistance which is another way she may achieve this privacy.

6.10. The need to be loved, to be needed, is fulfilling through the nurturance of a child. It is somebody to be responsible for. It is the most intense relationship known to humankind. In the rigors of life in the ghetto and the everyday difficulties in survival the presence of a child offers hope, promise, and somebody to be important for. In the social milieu of a large family, where the individual may feel sometimes unrecognized, the caring for a child intensifies the boundaries of a woman's identity and personality.

6.11. A woman desires a child because it offers the promise of a continuity of a close and intense relationship, while men may come and go (Aschenbrenner, p. 56), promising little that can compare to a mother's relationship to her child.

95

6.12. The bearing of a child for a woman is often an emotional elevation. At least, this is often the expectation of a woman anticipating a pregnancy. Continuous economic stress can foster depression and the bearing and nurturing of a child offers a woman a path out of the doldrums of the tedium of everyday routines (personal communications).

A final note on the causes of high fertility does not figure among the prominent variables, but, nevertheless, does manifest itself among a minor segment of the culturally disadvantaged of urban society: poor education about birth control. Among lower-class women who reside in Black ghettos (I also found this ignorance about birth control and the biology of reproduction to be present among poverty level Appalachians and Puerto Ricans), there is a decided ignorance about birth control and a short-sightedness about future burdens that may be a consequence of having children without adequate support. From this writer's own clinical experience, I have met young women of Black, Puerto Rican and Appalachian backgrounds, from extremely poor neighborhoods, who had not realized how they had become pregnant. Assuredly, these examples are exceptional, but nevertheless they exist.

7. Welfare Policy. The seventh major variable contributing to the matrifocal household is welfare policy. Specifically, a woman can be denied public assistance to herself and her children if she is found residing with a man. And, of course if the father of her children has no means of economic support he cannot reside with her without jeopardizing the support she gets from welfare.

8. Legal Pressure. The last variable to consider as contributing to the matrifocal family is the legal pressure that discourages a man from claiming paternity. To claim paternity obligates him to become responsible for that child. This becomes impossible when this father has no means of support. Income may be irregular and this could bring about continuous investigation by welfare authorities as to his financial status. It also adds to his own frustrations regarding his sense of

inadequacy in not being able to support his child. It is a threat to his masculinity which calls for his maneuvers to redefine his sense of identity and claim some measure of validity to his personhood through other means.

The matrifocal household, then, should not be considered a family unit, for her relationships to her personal kindred are what she considers her family. Matrifocality is a function of forces that are often beyond a person's control, male or female, and must be considered as a pattern of adaptation to a socioeconomic environment that frustrates the attainment of a family ideal.

The Androcentric Network

The fifth form of domestic organization is a function of the fourth, for if matrifocality is a social unit consisting of a woman living with, having responsibility for, and authority over her children, we must then account for the men. If a considerable segment of the male population is not heading up households and maintaining their roles as heads of family, then where are they? What is their status and function in the Black community?

The other side of the matrifocal coin is what I shall call the androcentric network of particularistic associations. Men maintain their own personal network of social relationships: with their personal kindred of parents and grandparents, brothers and sisters, aunts and uncles, nephews and nieces, and fictive kin; with their children and the mothers of their children; with current consorts and ex-consorts; with close male friends and socially more distant male associates; with all of whom they maintain reciprocity relationships of one form or another in a personal system of mutual competitive transaction or support or just simple intimacy. One important difference in men's relationships is that men are more mobile than women and men's relationships appear more fluid, more labile, than the relationships of women which are more centered and enduring with a relatively fixed number of family members. The more notable studies of the lifestyles and networks of Black men of the ghetto include Liebow (1967), Hannerz (1969), and Brown (1965).

The Extended Family

That larger group of people, connected by ties of blood and conjugal affiliation, maintaining a continuity of relationship through generations, has been the basis for human survival since the beginning of human existence, and probably before that. The nuclear family, which is so highly recognized in mainstream America, is just that--a nucleus. If we use the cell analogy for a moment we recognize that a nucleus does not exist by itself, but rather, maintains its viability in its relationship to its cell environment. Neither survives without the other. Similarly, the nuclear family is not very viable without a great deal of support, and traditionally, that environment of support has been the extended family. If anyone doubts the tenuous viability of the nuclear family one merely has to become familiar with the statistics on divorce, domestic violence, and child abuse to see that the general community support agencies do not provide anywhere near the support that a well-integrated extended family can offer. The American economy has fostered a nuclear family self-sufficiency among the mainstream middle classes, but this economic self-sufficiency has not necessarily provided a concomitant "moral fabric" (healthy relationships) of social organization that furthers human growth and development at all ages and among all classes and ethnic groups.

The Black extended family maintains a domestic network of widespread associations which are kept alive through the circulation of needed resources in money, material goods, and service. Maintained through a moral principle of reciprocal obligation with a high value placed on generosity, the pattern of "swapping" (Stack, p. 32ff) assures family members access to meager resources in time of need. The "mortar" of extended kin affiliations, then, is the importance of mutual support and the actual contributions each member makes to that domestic group. One's rights of membership in a domestic group is based upon that person's contributions to the group. It is the same principle that holds for the validation of parental rights whether or not the person in question is the biological parent.

The Black extended family is bilateral, recognizing members on both sides of the parents, and recognizing the in-laws of both spouses to a conjugal relationship. It is multigenerational, recognizing and incorporating parents, grandparents, and if they are living, great grandparents into the domestic group. And, the extended family also incorporates fictive kin who, although are not related by blood or marriage, have stood the test of time and have become as close as blood kin so as to be given a family title such as "auntie" or "uncle" or "brother" or "sister" or "mama."

Aschenbrenner has observed six key values that contribute to the culture of family life. These values are a) very strong consanguineal ties of reciprocal obligation and mutual support, b) an independent spirit with a high value on self-reliance (Kennedy also stresses the importance of this value), c) a strong emphasis on the importance of children who are or should be valued for their own sake, d) widespread and easy adoption of children, e) strong protective mothers, and f) a strict discipline with a considerable emphasis on one's respect for elders. This moral orientation is not just a phenomenon of urban Black communities of the north, but, in fact, is a reflection of a long tradition of family values reaching back to the beginnings of Black history in the rural south, and possibly, further back than that.

The Church-Oriented Community

The seventh order of social organization is the community. The concept of community commonly refers to an aggregation of people who share the same geographic area, such as a neighborhood, village, town, or suburb, share common rights and duties and interests and confront commonly shared problems as a unified group. The members of a community normally maintain civil and personable relationships with each other and assume a certain level of fellowship amongst themselves. The normal range of conflicts, disputes, and problems are handled by members in authority within that community. I would like to extend this concept of community a bit further to include persons connected through channels of communication who may not live within the geographical proximity of those members of the community that they identify with, but whose influence and contributions are acknowledged and whose association and presence is experienced at one time or another by the proximal members of that community.

The church has traditionally been the focus of Black community life. Frazier (1968) acknowledges that in the rural South the Black church was the most important realm of social organization and communality next to the family itself. In fact, the church community in both the rural South as well as the urban north often uses the idiom of the family to refer to those members of the church community. In the rural South it was relatively easy to maintain personalistic community ties amongst the members of a church community because of the smallness of the population and the rigid form of racial segregation that endured.

During W.W.I and after W.W.II substantial waves of Black migrations to the north took place. The primary motivations for these waves of migration were two: First, there was the increased availability of employment which was stimulated by the war effort. Second, there was the hope of escaping at least the hard edge of racial oppression experienced in the South; and for many there were wider hopes than that, as the expression "Promised Land" implied.

But, in the north, especially the urban north, a very different set of social and cultural circumstances obtained. The customary familistic mode of personal association was difficult to come by. The apparent anonymity of urban persons, the overwhelming variety of urban stimuli, intermix of different economic classes and ethnic groups of people, the life options one could choose from, and the fact that southern Blacks did not migrate from the South en masse, but came piecemeal, all these factors came together as a major crisis that required serious efforts at adaptation.

As Williams (1974) notes, those Black churches that were already established in the urban north left something to be desired for the newcomers. The well-established Black congregations of the North wanted nothing of the "back home" practices that could remind them of their subjugation. Then too, the urbanity of the northern Black churches, which practiced one or another form of European Protestantism, was alien to the rural newcomers. These migrants from the South, then, began forming their own separatist churches which attempted to recapture those attributes they were familiar with in the South. The dominant attraction in forming the separatist church was, as Fauset notes, their desire "to worship in churches where they could feel free to express themselves along the lines which the general condition of their lives prompted" (1971, p. 8). From these churches issued forth those agencies and functions that tied the Black community together: recreational programs, mutual aid associations, credit unions, educational cooperatives, music clubs, and fraternal organizations; and later, social, religious, and civil rights movements some of which grew to the national level of participation.

The multifunctional dimensions of the social organization of this Black church created a vitality and a durability that allowed it to become yet another institution of American society. Mays and Nicholson (1969), in their intensive two year study of the Negro church in America, point out several functions that contributed to this viability.

1. The church was one of the few, if not the only, public institution that was owned and controlled by its congregation. Possibly, the only other public institution to come close to this form of domain is the Lodge. For the many who cannot own their own home, the church has become the object of pride and investment. Even if the congregation were poor, as most were, and had incurred debts, the church was not and still is not easily liquidated; and usually, as the authors have shown, these debts were not great, and churches had a good reputation for eventually paying them off (Ibid. p. 279).

2. The complex level of social organization with its wide variety of activities provided opportunities for economic and social advancement. Since the church was controlled by its congregation, it not only provided members with opportunities as a religious institution, but also as a community-based center for economic and political activities (Ibid. p. 281). Both the religious-based activities and the secular endeavors provide avenues for the development of social status in the community and self-esteem for the individual.

3. The church provides leisure-time activities. Many Blacks feel more comfortable among their own than in a racially mixed social setting and the church provides this insulation and a greater freedom to relax. As the authors express it, the Negro lives in a racially tense environment and must be mindful of how he or she makes one's way in a white-dominated society. But within the church this tension can subside.

In many instances he expresses himself in song, dance and laughter, but for thousands of Negroes this release from restraint, this complete freedom and relaxation for the sake of mere expression, if nothing more than a faint 'Amen,' a nodding of the head as the minister preaches, a feeling of oneness with the crowd in song and prayer, is to be found only in the Negro church (Ibid. p. 283).

4. The church, as a community center, has the important function of acting as a vehicle for accessing other community agencies both within and outside of the Black community (Ibid., p. 285).

5. Many ministers encourage a commitment to education and business, exhorting their members to make sacrifices so that their children will have "a better day." Parents are thus called upon to volunteer their teaching skills in church education endeavors, and are asked for donations in supporting education in the church. For business the church is an important advertizing channel. Pastors advocate particular products and businesses to

patronize, insurance companies to buy from, and banks to save in (Ibid. p. 286).

6. Democratic fellowship is warmly welcomed among church members. Most churches have no social class distinctions. A dominant ideology preached in the church is to refrain from invidious social status distinctions and commune with each other as equals (Ibid. p. 287).

7. The Negro church endeavors to transcend racial barriers. The authors found in their study that many ministers and pastors are fighting against the racial divisions of society by preaching tolerance and accepting nonNegros, inviting white ministers and guest preachers, inviting white visitors, who are usually offered the best seats as a gesture of cordiality (Ibid. pp. 288-9). These social functions, then, further clarify how the church had been and still is the focus of Black community life.

But, as noted in chapter V, the church needs a leader if it is to be a viable and vibrant social community. The church leader in most cases is the nexus of religious community life and in many cases is the focal point of nonreligious or secular social activities as well. The role of the Black preacher has its origins in the earliest period of American history. Black preaching is primarily an oral tradition born in the context of slavery. Through the teachings of the Protestant slavemasters and religionists the American slaves became familiar with Protestantism. The new religion of the slaves was reinforced by the evangelizing of the missionaries (at first Anglican), and accompanying their learning of this new religion they went through their formal conversion. And emerging from the conversion process the slaves began speaking for themselves (Washington, pp. 65-7).

The tradition of Black preaching, from the very beginning, has maintained itself in the form of dialogue; a dialogue between the preacher and the congregation. A successful dialogue is possible because the preacher makes religion meaningful in the context of everyday experience. Mitchell (1970), an important

Black scholar and a clergyman for more than forty years, puts the following meaning on the role and significance of dialogue:

> Real dialogue...occurs characteristically in response to the preacher's reference to something that is vital in the life experience of the respondent-- something he identifies with, something which elicits his asseveration.
>
> He is able to respond because he is at home; he is interested in what the preacher is saying because he is involved, crucially involved in the issues as the preacher shapes them with scriptural reference and skillful allegory (p. 97).

The preacher's pragmatic orientation extends not only to the congregation but also to the Bible. Rather than seeing the Bible as an abstract code of doctrine and law, the Black preacher sees it as a unlimited source of good preaching material with which everyday experience can be cast within a more transcendent perspective (Mitchell, p. 113). The style of the Black preacher's delivery is unique in his emphasis of the pragmatic mode by speaking of the characters in the Bible as if he had a personal relationship with them; makes them living persons acting out the familiar concerns of the congregation (Ibid., p. 123). There is no doubt that in the Black church successful preaching is the craft of good story-telling.

But, if a preacher is to be successful in holding his congregation, for the duration of the service or for many years, he must be polished in the familiar style of traditional preaching. This style is more easily experienced directly than written about. But, Mitchell has delineated several aspects or features of Black preaching style (Ibid., pp. 162-176) that helps us understand the cultural distinctiveness of the Black church service. Suffice it here to list these features of Black preaching style.

1. _Personal style_. A preacher develops his own delivery. There is a wide range of styles and mannerisms that create that

style, but it is important that it fits the person delivering that sermon.

2. <u>The use of Black vernacular</u>. Black English is necessary to communicate on both the cognitive and emotional levels and is critical in moving the congregation. Black vernacular must remain the language of the church; the gospels will retain the rich meaning for the people only if they are delivered in the language and in terms of the people's culture.

3. <u>Permissive preaching</u>. A great deal of permissiveness in preaching allows the preacher a good deal of freedom in his development of a personal style. "To be themselves" Black congregations enjoy idiosyncratic mannerisms and the individuality that it expresses as well as celebrates.

4. <u>Musical tone or chant</u>. Variously referred to as "moaning," "mourning," "whooping," "tuning," or "zooning," it adds color and emphasis and drama to the sermon. Whether it is used just to emphasize a particular phrase or point or used throughout the sermon, there is no formula as to when to use it. It is "played by ear" by the preacher who senses the appropriateness of this device. A moaned message makes people "happy" and many feel a spirituality emanating from this mode of expression. Mitchell feels that intonation is not only an effective mode of communication style, but is also a mode of expression native to African peoples and therefore the moaning message harkens one back to his roots and his African identity. Intonation, as well as any other mannerism of preaching must be a genuine expression of the person. "You preach what the Spirit say you preach, and you do what the spirit say do!" (p. 173). Insincerity will kill the effectiveness of a sermon.

5. <u>Call-and-response</u>. The call-and-response pattern, otherwise known as the antiphonal dialogue is virtually universal in the Black church. All preachers must include opportunities for the congregation to respond. There are usually conventional places where the preacher may expect and receive response, and other points in the service where he will ask for it.

6. Repetition. Repetition of words, phrases, and sentences emphasize the point and add to the poetry of the deliverance. It expresses the preacher's concern that the intensity of the message has priority over the "extensity" of a message.

7. Role-playing. The preacher will pretend to be living in biblical times and will take on the role of a biblical character so as to personalize the point of a story told in a story-telling way.

8. Story-telling. This mode of deliverance is for the entertainment of it and because it frames the message emotionally and mythologically, pointing out classical mythological themes such as the importance and moral righteousness of the struggle against oppression and the quest for liberation.

9. Aphorisms. The use of aphorisms, or clever pithy statements, is not critical to one's tool kit of stylistic devices but is commonly used and responded to.

10. Stammering and hesitation. This mode of delivery attempts to impress upon the congregation that the preacher is struggling to hear the message from on high. He is groping for the Truth and motions in a pleading way for the holy spirit to put the right words into his mouth. He gives the congregation a feeling for the "weakness" of the preacher to which the congregation responds, recognizing their common oppression and vulnerability to society and to God. To the preacher's hesitation the congregation will shout "Help him, Lord!" This technique will also build suspense and increase interest in the emerging expression and message.

The Ethnic Group

Ethnicity refers to the furthest boundary demarcating the field of particularistic or familistic relations (Reminick, 1983). The term ethnic group does not actually refer to a group, which, technically is an aggregate of people in some form of ongoing significant association. Here, we are referring to a people who share a similar history and feel they have a common destiny, are distinguishable from other groups in terms of race, language, religion, and values; occupy an ascribed status in the wider society, and experience a certain communaute de conscience, a "we" feeling, a consciousness of kind that links members into an identifiable body of people and culture. John Gwaltney conceives Black ethnicity as "a nation within a nation" (1980, p.1). And, as Joseph Langstaff, one of Gwaltney's respondents, put it, "Black men have no country, but they are a country in their hearts" (Ibid.).

Ethnic Boundaries

Ethnic cultures can be conceived as having boundaries. These boundaries are defined by the forces that hold an ethnic group together. There is an analytical distinction being made between ethnic group and ethnic culture. The former refers to that population of persons maintaining social contact with each other and whose social behavior is relatively constant over time. The latter refers to mind phenomena, shared orientations and identities. Those forces that create a sense of boundary for an ethnic group are more formally recognized as the boundary maintaining mechanisms of ethnic culture. Three scholars who have identified these mechanisms of ethnic culture are Frederick Barth (1969) and LeVine and Campbell (1972). They were interested in identifying those forces and processes that maintain ethnic groups as identifiable entities. A fuller discussion of this phenomenon of ethnic culture can be found in Theory of Ethnicity (Reminick, 1983). Here, I have combined their particular contributions into 12 points. The first six points come from the contributions of LeVine and Campbell and the second six are from Barth.

1. A high degree of shared distinctive features that are part of the identity of an ethnic group and are most often ascribed through cultural tradition, make up the first boundary-maintaining mechanism. Within a cultural group there is a considerable amount of common sharing of physical, cultural, social, and psychological attributes among its members.

2. Members of an ethnic group have a high degree of proximity to each other. Persons maintain relatively close

distance to each other in space and time, forming communities geographically distinct from the larger society. Further, communication networks are maintained between persons and groups of the same ethnic persuasion in geographically distant areas.

3. A common history, a shared historical experience, and a sense of a common destiny, readily maintains patterns of identity amongst members of an ethnic group.

4. The mechanism of cultural pattern continuity refers to the conventionalization of patterns of behavior which remain relatively stable over time and tend to promote a consonance with patterns of thinking and values.

5. There is a considerable tendency for a greater intensity of communication to exist among the members of an ethnic group than between ethnic groups. The continuous exchange of ideas, feelings, and experience amongst the ethnic group members allows for a gradual process of adaptation to the larger society of which that ethnic group is a part.

6. Any recognizable social or ethnic group has a quality of boundary impermeability where a considerable amount of resistance is generated against the intrusion of sociocultural elements from outside the ethnic group that are considered foreign, unfamiliar, or in some way pose a threat to the integrity of the group. Items of the material world, especially items of technology are easily acquired, but values, especially religious and kinship values, attitudes about outgroups, or social customs meet with a considerable resistance since values and attitudes connect more deeply into basic ethnic personality structure than do the items of the material world which have much more pragmatic value.

7. Ascribed status is a strong determinant of ethnic cultural boundaries and identity. Ascribed status is given without the possibility of choice. Status value could be great or small, high or low, depending on the value system of that particular culture

in question. In some societies a great deal of status value is vested in a first-born son by families. In other societies a very low status is placed upon people who work with their hands; manual laborers who sweep streets, tan leather, or hammer iron. In European and American societies there is a great deal of status value distinctions placed upon the racial and ethnic groups that inhabit these regions. It is usually the ethnic groups of color upon which the politically dominant population imposes a low status value and thereby places limitations on the access that group has to the resources offered by the dominant population.

8. Population pressures that create demographic imbalances among the resident ethnic groups can intensify the differences between these groups engendering a variety of negative consequences, especially when there is a competition among these groups for society's critical resources.

9. Resource competition mobilizes various ethnic populations in their respective quests for scarce but necessary resources that allow for that group's survival and development of their living standards. When resources (e.g., jobs) are scarce, individuals must mobilize themselves into corporate groups that more efficiently wield power against other like-formed groups. The factor of ethnicity allows for easily formed lines of communication and organization since shared experience, shared culture, allows the orientation of familistic values (e.g., the recognition of "brothers" and "sisters") to extend to ethnic members not technically recognized as "family."

10. Adequate and effective role performance of ethnic group members at the levels of family and community is vital in maintaining cultural boundaries and in competing adequately for scarce vital resources available in the wider society. The most critical form of role performance with regard to resource competition is political. Social behavior that maximizes one's chances for accessing political power enhances the viability of the ethnic group as a whole and heightens one's ethnic and personal status.

11. The adequate satisfaction of identity needs reinforces the ethnic group identity and thus the boundaries of that group. Identity need satisfaction derives from the consequences of political effectiveness, economic access, and the freedom to achieve particularly desired ethnic and personal goals. This normally facilitates a secure and relatively stable domestic group organization which, in turn, provides a foundation for adequate personality development and a commitment to the cultural ideals and goals of that group. This normally feeds back upon and nourishes one's personal identity thereby satisfying the need.

12. Endemic in most complex and pluralistic societies today and throughout history are the mechanisms of political discrimination and oppression which effectively isolate a group from the rest of society and which are counted among the externally-imposed forces of cultural boundary maintenance.

PART THREE

SOCIALIZATION AND PERSONALITY

Introduction

In the following chapters I will describe several theoretical models that will help the reader conceptualize the internal dynamics of a) the processes of socialization, b) personality and its developmental stages, and c) Black identity. In doing this I shall also demonstrate the conceptual relationships between these functional processes. Thus, the way a child is reared and taught will have a great influence upon the nature of the personality that develops. And, the particular components and dynamics of a person's personality will feed into the nature of that person's ethnic, in this case, Black, identity.

Before proceeding with the development of these models for the understanding of Black psychosocial identity a few postulates need to be made explicit. Postulates are scientific assumptions that few scientists would choose to argue about anymore. They usually involve recurrent observations coming out of a variety of studies over long periods of time with little change in their information value. For example, in the '40's Miller and Dollard hypothesized that frustration generated aggression in most mammals. It was known as the frustration-aggression hypothesis. Experiments were carried out with a variety of animal species from rats on up to the primates and including human beings. This once-called hypothesis is now considered something of a law and has been elaborated to considerable extents in the behavioral sciences, especially psychology. I shall be using a variation of this model later on.

The first postulate I wish to note is that culture and personality are analytical categories. That means that you can make analytical distinctions within the phenomenon you are observing, but the reality makes these distinctions indivisible. My point here is that personality cannot be understood without knowing the culture from which that personality is developed. That culture is the information and value that functions as the basic building blocks of personhood. Therefore, any psychological study of Black personality that doesn't seriously consider the content of that person's cultural life is going to fall short of understanding Black personality dynamics. This issue must be a particularly sensitive one, especially among Black psychologists, because one sees little more than a consideration of such issues as cognitive functioning, assertiveness, achievement motivation, self-esteem, mental health problems, and still, very frequently, defense of the equality and the equal value of the Black race, with African institutions brought in to bolster the argument. The problem is that although these areas are important to consider they offer only a skeletal construct of personality and there is very little in that to distinguish these problems from a good number of other ethnic groups, especially those of the lower social classes.

My second postulate to note is a response to those investigators who feel it still necessary to prove that Blacks are cognitively as intelligent as whites. Anthropologists and cross-cultural psychologists doing studies all over the world for several generations now have demonstrated that the human species evolved a common brain with an enormous range of performance ability. And, we find in most cultures studied, that there is a certain range of variation in cognitive performance within any ethnic group that takes the statistical shape of the bell curve with the modal population registering within a normal range of variation and with minority cohorts on each end; one end representing a below normal intellectual functioning and the other end registering an abnormally high intellectual functioning. Each ethnic population, then, has the potential to have members that span the range from severely retarded on through to the very brilliant and, although somewhat rare, the genius.

My third postulate is that every ethnic population of the human species represents a range of variation of personality types. This range of variation within an ethnic group is greater than the differences one would find between ethnic groups. Therefore, anyone who attempts to generalize about an ethnic personality type is treading on unstable ground and inviting the danger of stereotyping the group in question. However, there is a way to grapple with this disconcerting problem and that is with the statistical concept of the modal personality. This refers to the fact that every ethnic population has certain common traditions, customs, history, and preferred ways of rearing children. Therefore, those patterns of behavior that are held in common by a significant segment of the population will have likewise similar personality functioning, especially if those patterns held in common are childrearing patterns which are critical in building particular types of personality.

The fourth postulate is that there is a dual modal personality organization; that there are important differences between male personality structure and female personality structure, and to lump these two categories into a general "Black personality" loses a great deal of the picture, especially the energy of the sexual dialectic that is a dominant factor in Black culture, social organization, and personality.

Part III, then, presents the issue of human development in general and the development of Black personality in particular. The chapter on socialization presents a general model for the context and development of the socialization process. Then, for the particulars, we focus down on a very specific Black socialization pattern that is functionally related to our general model. In the chapter on personality configurations I present motivational models that help explain some dominant Black personality characteristics, of males and of females, pointing out some of the causal conditions for the difference. In the chapter on personality I note those important features of Black ethnicity that members of this ethnic culture espouse as important for their own personal identity as Black Americans.

VII

THE SOCIALIZATION PROCESS

Socialization is a learning process. It involves both cognitive and emotional learning as well as conscious and unconscious learning. Cognitive learning is the acquisition of information and categories of information that organize the world for a person and imbues that world with meaning, order, and value. Cognition most often refers to thinking, reasoning and problem solving which become accessible through and transmitted by language. Emotional learning involves the emotional response to particular categories of person, place, or event. Children's emotional responses towards other people include such things as love, respect, awe, loyalty, joking equality, intimacy, hostility or fear. The response is most often a function of the context of a situation and the nature of the relationship and treatment of the child. Early learning normally has a great emotional endurance through time because much of it is beyond the grasp of language and memory. In this respect the cognitive learning of children is much more mutable and amenable to change. Much cognitive learning, for example, learning proper social conduct, occurs at the conscious level through intentional instruction by the socializers. But, even here so much information is accumulated that most of it goes into what psychoanalysts call the "preconscious," to be recalled when needed. On the other hand, emotional learning is largely unconscious. We respond to particular persons or categories of person, such as an authority figure, and are aware of how we feel toward them, but may not really understand how we came to learn what we feel at particular times in particular relationships. Socialization is the learning of habitual and conventional ways of behavior in social situations. Although the major amount of learning occurs in childhood, novel or changing situations in adulthood may necessitate relearning social conduct on both the cognitive and the emotional levels.

A Systems Model of Human Adaptation

Whiting and Child (1953) conceived a model of human adaptation that placed human socialization into a larger perspective than what is usually found within the discipline of psychology. Their scheme involved six levels of operation. At

Environment

a. terrain
b. climate
c. flora
d. fauna

-->

Innate Biology

a. organic structures
b. instincts
c. drives
d. basic needs
e. potentials

Social Maintenance Institutional Systems

-->

a. subsistence patterns
b. settlement patterns
c. kinship and descent
d. economic system
e. political organization

Socialization Institutions

-->

a. methods of
   teaching
b. modes of
   learning
c. discipline
d. task

assignments
e. initiation/
   puberty
   rites

the first level are the independent variables, i.e., those conditions that human beings have little or no control over and which heavily influence the nature of human adaptation. These conditions are the physical environment and innate biology. The physical environment includes a) terrain (mountains, valleys, plains, etc.), b) climate, c) flora (plant life), and d) fauna (animal life). Innate biology includes a) the organic structures of the body, b) instincts, c) drives, d) the basic needs, and e) the potentials of the self.

The second level of operation is the social maintenance system. At this level human groups evolve institutions, i.e., ongoing systematic patterns of organized behavior, that allow them to survive and grow in their particular environment. These social institutions include a) subsistence patterns (modes of gathering resources for survival and adaptation), b) settlement patterns (whether highly dispersed or densely grouped), c) kinship and descent systems for the organization of domestic corporate groups, d) economic systems of production, distribution, and consumption of necessary resources, and e) political organization for the development of bases of power.

116

Child Personality and Child Peer Group Culture	Adult Personality and Modal Character	Projective/ Expressive Symbol Systems
-->	-->	
a. modes of thought		a. myth/legend/ proverb
b. games		b. religion
c. childhood beliefs, fears		c. magic
		d. ritual
		e. art
		f. recreation
		g. deviance/ pathology

Diagram 7.1

It is at the third level of operation where our present concerns become focused, where we place the institutions of socialization. Institutions of socialization, then, are adaptive responses to survival in a particular physical, social, and cultural environment. Socialization functions to orient, condition, and guide the neonates of society (the children) in maintaining those institutions that survive their group from generation to generation. Getting the children of a population to commit themselves to carrying on time-proven values and patterns of behavior require a) specific methods of teaching, b) particular modes of learning, c) patterns of discipline consistent with a group's behavioral requirements, d) task assignments, and e) certain rituals that dramatize the importance of doing what is required and that provide for the enactment of transition phases from one stage of maturation to the next.

The fourth level of operation is a consequence of the third, as the second level is of the first. It is the configuration of child personality and peer group culture. At this level we take into consideration a) modes of child thought, which often includes magical thinking and a whole lot of fantasy, b) the

117

games of girls and boys that often act out the roles they are being trained for, and c) childhood beliefs and fears and the legends, stories, and child folklore that symbolize these beliefs and fears.

At the fifth level we have the adult modal personality. Normally, a significant segment of the society or ethnic group, if not a majority, who experienced the dominant socialization patterns and whose child personalities developed normally out of those socialization experiences, carry out traditional roles and perpetuate adaptive values and beliefs that contribute to the ongoing solidarity of their group. In some societies, where rapid social change is going on, it is not time-worn traditions that are encouraged, but rather, innovative thinking and behavior that is oriented to the problems for which traditional methods have no solutions.

At the final level of operation are the cultural systems of symbolic expression; systems of thought, feeling, and value that express the experience of survival and adaptation. These systems of creative expression include a) myth, legend, and proverb, b) religion, c) ritual, d) magic, e) art, f) science, g) recreation, and h) deviance and pathology which are maladaptive, if not destructive, modes of expressing the stress of particular situations and ongoing conditions of life.

Ethnographic Case 1: The Situational Context

Moving from the general to the particular, I wish to present an ethnographic case that demonstrates how a pattern of socialization creates a training ground for a child's adaptation to the real world. This case is not generally representative of the Black socialization experience in America. It is however a widespread pattern most highly represented among matrifocal households of Black America. It is a pattern commonly found in households on public assistance and within communities of the working poor.

This particular study of Black socialization (Young, 1976) succinctly demonstrates in microcosm what is found in the

macrocosm of the wider society. Young's study reveals the
lessons, the modes of adaptation, a child must learn within the
confines of the domestic group that will help that child survive
and adapt as an adult. The microcosm of Young's study is a day
care center where a pattern of socialization observed had
operating within it the major rules and orientations needed, i.e.,
the cultural tools, to make some form of adaptation in their, the
children's, society when they became adults. This study focused
on a day care center in a Black community of Chicago. I will
summarize the study here.

The study was oriented to understanding the differences
between the Black and white behavioral patterns of socialization.
The major hypothesis used was that the Black socialization
pattern should be significantly different from that of the white
middle class. The assumption is that if a Black child did learn a
white middle class pattern it would prove inadequate for that
child within the Black community because the teaching of
standard conventional values would be maladaptive in navigating
through the daily encounters of Black community life. Young
gives three reasons why this should be so: First, Black
Americans participate in two spheres of American culture: Black
culture and the standard American or white dominated culture.
For this reason Black Americans are bicultural. Second, Black
Americans continually experience extensive discrimination and
economic privation. And third, Black Americans live with the
ongoing struggle and hope for social change that will win for
them a greater equality in American society.

Young, then, articulates four primary objectives of her study.
They are, first, to observe, on the one hand, the parent figures
teaching the children certain techniques of adaptation to persons
as well as to the situations that these authority figures imposed
upon the children, while on the other hand, observing how these
children maintain their own strong sense of independence vis-a-
vis the persons in authority, who often were their own mothers.
The second objective was to analyze how this adaptive strategy
developed through the mother-child relationship. Third, to
understand how these children learned their mother's disposition

119

toward them and how they learned to adapt to their mother's imposed demands while at the same time not losing sight of their commitment to their own personal goals. And fourth, to understand the general cognitive problem for these children which is in dealing with two sets of directions, those of the authority figure and those of one's self.

Two dominant themes stand out in observing and analyzing the socialization pattern in this day care center. The first is the mother's authority which is imposed arbitrarily along with the use of corporal punishment. The second theme is that of the mother encouraging the child's sense of autonomy from the mother's authority. Although these two themes appear contradictory to each other, their function, which becomes clear in the analysis, is significant in the context of the wider society.

Close examination of parent-child interaction revealed that corporal punishment was commonly and swiftly resorted to in the management of the child's behavior. But, it was used inconsistently and arbitrarily. Sometimes the mother rapped the child for doing something and other times she didn't. Interestingly, the child's responses of crying and subsequent behavior were not emotionally charged. In a white middle class authoritarian context the child commonly becomes hostile, resentful, or withdrawn. In the Black situation the child did not sulk or withdraw, but rather, watched the mother's mood changes.

The mother is observed as structuring the relationship in the form of a contest in which the mother appears to enjoy the child's truculent and spirited resistance. The child responds to the mother's domination by challenging her and threatening to do what he or she was punished for doing previously. In this dialogue the mother and the child become playful and alert to the behavior of each other.

So, what are the implications of this pattern of behavior? The contest establishes a relationship of equality, rather than one of dominance and submission, the latter of which is commonly

found in the white working class family. The child is expected
to pursue his or her own purposes and both mother and child
employ ingenuity and persistence in achieving their own ends.
Now, the mother remains clearly dominant and the child must
accept her authority, but, the child's own autonomy is not
attacked. In the standard authoritarian household there is a
pattern of dominance and submission and the child must withdraw
because because of anger or guilt. The Black child experiences
not only his or her mother's enjoyment of the contest but also
the mother's encouragement of the child's autonomy.

Because of the inconsistency and arbitrariness of punishment,
a child learns that an act punished at one time may not be
punished at a later time if that act is repeated. This
arbitrariness of the mother's authority reveals that she is
exerting her own personal authority and not the authority of
some abstract code. The question of right or wrong is only
secondary in this context. What is important, what the child is
really learning, is that the mother is being dominant at a
particular time. Actions of the child were punished not because
what the child did was necessarily wrong, but because it simply
was not permitted at the moment. In this context, then, the
children are not learning a moral code of conduct. Followers of
standard white middle class culture might find this disconcerting
because these children are not necessarily learning right from
wrong, but rather, are learning what they can get away with and
when. In the observations of mothers in the day care center the
mothers did not take a moralistic stand, as would be the case in
the standard American cultural context, but rather, they simply
asserted their momentary domination. Neither did adults normally
make judicial decisions in mediating relationships between the
children. Rather, the children handled their own interpersonal
relations with a sensitivity to the group that far exceeded that
of white middle class children. (The author has done comparative
studies of both white and Black parent-child interactional
patterns.)

The Black English term "bad" becomes important here because
being "bad" is both condemned and admired by children and

adults alike. The term "bad" refers to the quality of self-assertiveness and this quality of behavior may be good or bad depending on the context of the situation and the consequences of this kind of behavior. Very assertive children often became disruptive in the group if what they were doing interfered with the group's activity at the time. But, of course, this assertive behavior would be praised when it furthered the activities of the group or the goals of the mothers in charge.

Thus, we may conclude this portion of the analysis by noting that this socialization process does not teach rules, but rather, it teaches procedures of interpersonal interaction involving both adaptation and manipulation.

To focus down now quite concretely in order to give the reader a sense of what was being observed I will quote two sample observations given by the investigator. The first case is an example of a dependent and frustrated boy being maneuvered by his mother into greater independent activity.

When he first appeared in my notes one morning, five-year-old James was provoking attention by pretending to run out the exit alley, by hitting a mother who was not his own, and by snatching toys twice in quick succession. His mother paid no attention until he snatched a jack-in-the-box from another child; his mother took it away from him and returned it to the other child. James began to throw a tantrum. His mother showed no reaction and the tantrum continued; James stood with his back to a wall, screaming. His mother picked up a large wet ball and dried it off in a desultory way. James, crying, followed her at a distance as she walked and continued to dry the ball. James was distracted by an unrecorded incident which he watched quietly for a few moments, then went stamping and crying to his mother who bounced the ball and kept it away from him, while she walked and talked to others. James continued to cry for the ball and leaned on his mother. His four-year-old brother was into mischief, but the mother

122

seemed not to notice. James continued to lean on his mother and soon stopped crying and smiled. His mother noticed the smile, then went to the four-year-old son and disciplined him. James whined, went after her, and leaned on her. She bounced the ball and yelled at him, "Shut up." The teacher passed by, saying of James, "Mrs. ---, that's your baby." James looked up at his mother. His mother cooed at another woman's baby, then played ball with an unrelated girl while restraining James from catching the ball with her other hand. Next James' mother picked up the jack-in-the-box. Several children reached for it, including James who cried hard for it. His mother gave it to James and her four-year-old son who both sat down quietly with it. They played for less than a minute when James left, and his brother continued to play with it. James joined a group of friends and did not return to his mother.

The author makes analytical comments in her field notes:

This mother's behavior was not in response to a specific infraction of rules but to James' general mood. He knew he should not snatch toys and a moral lesson was not her intent; instead she guided his mood, playfully teasing him until his tantrum was over; then she teased him more strongly, punishingly, in order to show her displeasure. After she had guided him out of his tantrum and disciplined him, she rewarded him with the object he had snatched in the beginning. An apparent resolution was reached, for James began independent activity (pp. 409-10).

This next scene, at lunch, between a four-year-old girl, Michele, and her mother, illustrates the pattern of the verbal contest that was so often observed in the day care center.

Twelve children were sitting at desks in groups of four facing each other, eating and being served by two mothers. Michele refused her mother's order to wash

her hands. Mother and child spent several minutes
alternately repeating the order and refusing; the mother
was casual about it and attended to the other children's
lunch trays. Michele's mother then reversed her position
and told her disinterestedly:

"Get in the chair and eat."
"I have to wash my hands."
"O.K., go wash your hands."

Michele went off sulkily, turned back after a few steps,
then went firmly to the washroom. She came back
drying her hands and eyes with a paper towel, went to
her mother, and finding her occupied, sat down near
her. The mother moved slowly around the room while
she and her daughter called back and forth to each other
in a leisurely, even paced, and rhythmic dialogue:

"Mama, I don't like this."
"You don't like what? Well leave it there on the plate,
I don't want it either."
"Mama, I want to put it in the garbage."
"yes?"
"Mama, I want to put it in the garbage."
"We don't got no garbage here." Mother takes it from
her.
"Mama, here, Mama, look down here." Michele points to
the spilled milk of her neighbor, Doreen.
"Yeah, I see. Every day she does the same thing.
Every day."
"Mama, here." Michele shows her a handful of
squeezed string beans. "Mama, look Mama."
"You want me to take you to the bathroom?"
"No."
"If you don't want something, leave it on your plate."
The mother is only casually the instructor and the
supervisor. Mother and child verbally contend over the
rules of eating. They both alternately threaten and

124

comply, and they express their mutuality in the
continuing conversation (p. 410).

We can conclude from this study, as Young does, that this
pattern of socialization is an adaptation to a bicultural situation
within which a Black person lives. Living in two different
cultural worlds can be stressful because a) the group may become
ambivalent or even divided regarding which role in society to
play, which system of values to espouse, and b) the personality
can become divided or split by being pulled in two different
directions, into the intimacy of the ethnic group or the power
superiority of the mainstream society, if one has the chance.

This socialization pattern, then, acts to resolve any potential
ambivalences and internal personality contradictions by focusing
on the maintenance of ego integrity and social identity in the
face of a society which imposes discrimination. The socialization
pattern focuses on "sizing up" persons and situations, constraints
and opportunities, and then, the child learns to act on his or her
own personal goals, getting what one can out of a particular
situation or person.

The outsider, such as a person of the white middle class,
may see this as a disregard for societal norms and even a
flaunting of the law. But, in the Black situation, one's personal
goals are to get around the norms and the laws that impose
discrimination.

Those patterns of behavior oriented to teaching children
preferred modes of conduct are not necessarily conscious choices
and intended plans of parental figures. Patterns of socialization
in any human group arise or evolve in response to many different
forces, including human biological predispositions, course of
history, social, economic, and political conditions of a particular
moment, and modal consensus of the group. The multitude of
choices and decisions made each day which form patterns in
rearing a child are enacted beneath the level of conscious
awareness and arise more from intuitive wisdom generated by

125

modes of communication and the sharing of experience among the members of an ethnic group.

This socialization pattern, then, is a function of a social organization based on the necessity for maintaining a considerable amount of flexibility while encountering adverse conditions of daily life. It is a social organization that is responsive to change when the conditions and opportunities are right. This is the Black community's adaptation to the white dominated society.

In conclusion, I must note that the ethnographic case elaborated here is an example of the poverty level of community life. It does not necessarily exemplify the socialization patterns of the working middle classes of Black communities. We can assume, however, that as economic resources become more accessible to members of the Black community the life style and social organization will approach that of mainstream America, yet will maintain many important Black traditions that have been elaborated earlier. This ethnographic example of a socialization process did not cover one very important factor and that is religion and the church. Although the data is sparse on the socialization influence of the church and religion on Black children, we must recognize it and point it out as an important field for further research.

Ethnographic Case 2: The Life History
I now provide an example of a socialization process in a wider context. Moving from the matrifocal socialization of young children in a restricted setting to the socialization of older boys and men in the context of their city, along some critical phases of the life course, we find an uncommonly rich source in Claude Brown's Manchild in the Promised Land (1965). The historical setting is the late '40s and early '50s in Harlem, New York. The social scene is not very different today, except that Brown himself sees the Harlem of the '80s in a relatively deteriorated cultural condition. Here, I can only highlight a few of those experiences that mark the forces and the course of socialization

for Brown in the Harlem ghetto and point out the harshness and brutality of life caused by racism, discrimination, and poverty.

It is an environment of stark contrasts. From the very beginning Harlem was fostered by a southern rural culture and fundamentalist religion and morality. In contrast to this there is the fast-moving street life with its own standards of right and wrong and its own basis for status and respect; where illegal involvements are the accepted modes for making a living. The educational system is seen by the children as alien and offering no promise of future reward. The opportunities for employment call for menial jobs with inadequate pay and promise low status and subservience. And the police, the agents and representatives of white domination, were, and still are, seen more as the forces of harrassment than as protection. And yet, Brown's community is vibrant with the music, dance, and the drama of Black culture, and the legendary Apollo Theater is looked upon as the touchstone for Black talent.

The social experience of Harlem boys was one of continual challenge. One of the first things a poor boy had to learn was to defend what he possessed, the most important of which included his money, his women, and his masculinity. At an early age Brown was strongly encouraged to fight for these prized possessions. His father taught Brown to face physical combat or get a beating when he returned home. Beatings from Brown's father were familiar to him and Brown learned that running from a fight meant running forever and thus losing any claim on those few things he could call his own.

Hardened by violence boys learned self-sufficiency through aggression. For those whose parents did not provide a home life the streets became their primary domicile and they fended for themselves. Boys had no problem staying out for days at a time, prowling the neighborhood finding things to steal and sell in order to provide for their needs and build a reputation.

Brown, like most other Harlem boys, rarely attended school. To be "cool" was to stay away from school. The streets were the classroom and the older hustlers were their teachers. They learned how to deal in drugs, the black market, and prostitution. Through these pursuits street life offered acceptable status and respect as compared to a "regular job" which was both unrewarding and humiliating.

But the parents, especially the mothers, were terribly naive about the exigencies of the peer group of boys. Parents of Brown's day knew mainly of the restricting, low-paying jobs and the church. Because of this there arose a definite schism between the generation of children and their parents. Brown's comment, "My mother's a fool" expresses his consternation about his mother's inability to understand what the life of the streets is all about. Children could not meet the expectations of their parents and parents could only grow more frustrated.

A major turning point in Brown's life occurred with his introduction to reform school. Sooner or later, it appeared, a boy would get caught for one thing or another and would be sent to reform school. A boy would experience this with some ambivalence because the street life was one of constant pressure and challenge and running and reform school was a cessation of the conditions of stress. It was for Brown a refuge. There, boys could "cool down" and evaluate their situation, make new friends, and even avail themselves of the influence of their counselors.

While at Warwyck School Brown became introduced to the world of books by Mrs. Cohen and his reading greatly broadened his horizons. Although still too young to see his way out of the Harlem life, dreams of a new way of life appeared much more feasible to him. Another reform school authority figure, Mr. Papanek, director of Wiltwyck School, became Brown's confidant and inspired Brown with new aspirations through Papanek's unwavering confidence in Brown's potential. Although Brown could not understand it, he noticed that several of his reform school counselors had an abiding faith in his ability to succeed; and this caused Brown to have a high regard for them, and also a growing regard for himself. This influence stayed with him after leaving these schools.

Brown returned to the life of constant tension generated by a futile way of life, most often ending in prison or death by murder or drug overdose. Brown, and his friends who were still alive, were no longer children chasing excitement but men and women whose chase often ended in tragedy. The experience of everyday deprivation was soothed by drugs and many became addicted to their anaesthetic which brought its own form of pain. Many of Brown's friends became swallowed by the fear that the pain they felt would continue forever. They feared that they would soon be unable to cope or change or be unable to accept any other way of life. Heroin swept over the youth of Harlem like a plague. Life became more strained for everyone, for the addicts in need made no distinctions between family, friend, or passing stranger. Anyone was a potential target for robbery and murder.

A critical turning-point for Brown in this maelstrom of events was during his successful marijuana business when he became the mark for a holdup. According to the rules of Harlem he had no choice but to buy a gun and kill his robber in order to regain his status in the community. Luckily, someone else killed the man first and freed Brown from that onerous obligation. This incident was cause for serious reflection. He made two decisions at this point: never to kill anyone and never to go to prison. It was for these reasons that he left Harlem.

But, he had built a very respectable reputation and therefore could return to Harlem without difficulty. No one could question his courage or bother him about his "going straight." His interest in music, which was born at Warwyck School, blossomed in Greenwich Village where he learned to play jazz piano. This was a sure road away from the dead-ends that waited for many a Harlem youth.

Claude Brown's autobiography is more than the story of his life. It is, in anthropological parlance, an ethnography, for it tells not only the story of one man, but the story of a community and a whole generation of boys who grew up in that community. And, as such, there is good reason to believe that one can generalize the themes in Claude Brown's story to many Black ghettos around the country. As an ethnography it is a story that is amenable to analysis; analysis of the forces that acted to create Claude Brown's socialization experience.

The following socialization experiences are not necessarily listed in their order of priority. The first two were primarily parental influences: discipline and nurturance. Brown discusses his discipline at the hands of his father. We can conclude that this discipline was arbitrarily meted out, was corporal in nature, and can be considered extra-punitive, if not abusive at times. But, the father's harshness was a response to the pressures of the environment which were harsh, and survival, sheer physical survival, depended upon toughness and the ability to withstand many different forms of shock. We may surmise then that Brown's father was responding adaptively in disciplining his son the way he did, so that Brown could withstand the harshness that he met in the streets. The psychoanalyst may also add that the father very well may have been using Claude Brown as a target of displacement of accumulated anger. Another motivation of the father, which was also dramatized in the film, "Nothing But A Man," was that Brown may have been a symbolic reminder of the father's own inability to properly care for his son because of the lifelong poverty of the ghetto; and this painful symbolic experience caused the father to aggress against the source of his sense of painful failure, which was his son, Claude.

In contrast to this we find the nurturance of Brown's mother, naive to the life of the streets and caring and worrying and wishing to be able to protect him from the trouble he might get himself into. (Her worry was not without reason, since on the very first page of the book Brown is shot in the stomach.) It is also interesting to read Brown's comments on a boy's response to nurturance. It is one of unresponsiveness, muteness. Not out of a lack of concern or involvement; not because a boy is not moved by nurturance, but because to be cool is to be outwardly unresponsive. This is an adaptive response because to get emotional is to lose control in situations that call for cool, calculated, and quick responses to potentially life-threatening situations.

Independence training is seen in numerous incidents; that emphasis on the value and quality of self-reliance, oft-times elaborated in other ethnographic studies of Black communities. It certainly was apparent in Brown's relationship to his father, but it was also an emphatic theme of training within the peer group.

The dominant theme elaborated in the story is the influence of the peer group. The peer group often became the source of the structure of a boy's social life and personality. It ruled the course of events in a boy's day and determined, for many, a boy's destiny after growing into a man. The peer group determined patterns of aggression a boy learned and lived, the nature of male-male social relations, the structure of masculinity and masculine identity, and patterns of subsistence; all of which we will touch upon in this section.

The school system was another source of socialization influence. Actually we can count two institutional school systems that were relevant in Brown's life. First, was the public school system that acted as an anti-influence in that that was the place not to go to. It was alien to the concerns of Harlem boys; the teachers were alien to their interests, and the public school represented itself as an agent of the oppressive society. Second, was the reform school, and this system was very influential in Brown's life, to the extent that it marked a turning-point, a crisis, charting new directions that Brown, at a later time embarked upon.

The punitive institutions, jails, prisons, and holding places for juvenile offenders, held out promise of what to expect when engaging in activities for which many of these boys had no alternatives. It was do what the gang did or be punished by them; and risk getting caught and punished by the punitive agency. Therefore, this institution vis-a-vis the gang put Brown "between a rock and a hard place."

The police represented another socialization influence, symbolizing the oppression of society with their frequent harassment of gang members and disregard for ghetto-dwellers in general. The police helped these boys forge their attitudes not only toward the police themselves but toward the society which the police represented.

Girls were another socialization influence, especially after boys became pubescent, but often, long before that. Girls were persons to protect and to defend; were objects to exploit; were challenges to the masculinity of boys; girls inspired boys to fall in love and diverted their loyalties from their male peers. Girls became women and continued to shape the lifestyle and decisions of the men of Harlem. Attitudes toward women were divided. There was the attitude of reverence that was normally held toward mother-figures. In Brown's case it was his own mother who was very nurturant and protective of him. Mrs. Meitner, the German lady of Wiltwyck School was Brown's confidant. Brown fell in love with her--she treated him with dignity. And then there was Mrs. Cohen who introduced him to the world of books which marked a major turning-point in his life by opening up a world Brown had here-to-fore been ignorant of. Other girls and women of Harlem whom one respected and protected included one's sisters, or to a lesser degree, the mates of one's brothers or fellow peer group members.

Then there were the women who were the objects of sexual involvement. A true love relationship developed with a Jewish woman which was cut short by her parents. Brown had many casual sexual relationships through whom he demonstrated certain aspects of his masculinity. Attitudes toward the opposite sex can be seen in the expression "women are bitches, men are dogs." One has to look out for women because they can take advantage of you. Women can be dangerous; they can betray you. They must be controlled; ruled, the way a pimp governs his "ladies." Men are dogs: They are always rutting around, playing the stud, on the prowl, running together in packs. Such was the way heterosexual attitudes were characterized in the streets of Harlem.

A cause as well as a consequence of socialization were the characteristics of masculinity that were played out on a day-to-day basis. These masculine characteristics included an emphasis on domination, aggressiveness and tactics of aggression, protection and defense of personal possessions, and sexual consorting. Reading Brown's story finds definitions of masculinity not too different from what other authors find in their studies. For example, Hannerz, in his study of street life in the ghetto of Washington, D.C., found masculinity to be defined by a high value on verbal skills and the ability for manipulation, toughness and the ability to command respect, personal appearance and high style, strong overt concerns with sexual exploits, and a propensity for liquor consumption. As Hannerz himself has pointed out, none of these traits contradict the mainstream definitions of masculinity. But, what is different is the emphasis and value put on these particular traits and the submersion of other traits defined by mainstream society, such as steady employment and family responsibility, aspects of life that the poor ghetto-dweller cannot live up to because of his position in society, but nevertheless has no less regard for than his white counterpart.

Patterns of aggression play a dominant part in Claude Brown's story, especially as learned behaviors of survival and the maintenance of status and respect. No less than six different forms of aggression can be analyzed out of Brown's life history; each form having a different function in shaping his social relationships and his attitude toward people.

One of the more common forms of aggression found among adolescent gang members is retaliatory aggression. This is usually acted out in the context of inter-gang warfare, either between whole groups or individual members of opposing gangs. Or, as the first scene in Brown's book illustrates, retaliatory aggression may be acted out by a potential victim against a real or suspected crime being committed. Retaliatory aggression is usually physical and violent. It is acted out in anger in terms of defense or offense and may be carefully premeditated or spontaneous and impulsive.

The most important form of aggression functioning to maintain a structure of social organization in the peer group of the streets was (and still is among contemporary street groups) what I will call aggressive domination. In many primate groups, including both the infra-human and human groups, we find patterns of domination using the aggressive mode which establishes a particular kind of social order, a pecking order, within the group. Comparing Claude Brown's peer group to infrahuman groups is not to devalue or derrogate the nature of adolescent peer group organization; it is an existential statement; it just is. This type of social organization is widespread among the primates. It is simple, direct, and oriented to the powerful individuals (seen in terms of both strength and intelligence) assuming the role of leadership.

It is a survival-oriented social organization that leaves little room for higher-level cultural pursuits. In this social context the fight is a test to establish social rank, to maintain a basis of power, a basis for establishing a sense of self-esteem. The stronger members of the group gain access to greater material and human rewards and the weaker members move to the margins of the peer group; but they are not rejected. The code of aggressive domination requires that each member fight. In this way the abilities of each member is known. It is the basis of friendship and trust in one's mutual defense of the other. As Brown has recounted in his story, the grounds for true egalitarian friendship are established between two equally-matched boys who cannot defeat each other. This creates a bond of loyalty; it is a pair-bond where each can call the other "brother" with a special feeling of fraternal intimacy.

This form of aggression is not limited to the males within the peer group. Girls, and later, women, are subject to aggressive domination as well. Certainly not a preferred mode of treatment for most women, males feel both a peer pressure to treat women aggressively and with dominance and also are internally motivated to do so for reasons I shall bring out later. The notions that guys are supposed to "treat girls like dirt," that they should be "pushed around," that sometimes they needed to "get beat up;" these were cultural prescriptions that Claude Brown learned in the school of the streets. But we also know that he found other ways of relating to women as well. And we have strong clues that his friends and street teachers also knew and had other ways of relating to women, but it was something private; something to be kept a cherished secret between a guy and his loved one.

Another form of domination involving an aggressive act in response to the infraction of a norm or the disobedience of a status superior, is identified as authoritarian aggression. It is found in the corporal punishment of parent against child, the beatings a gang leader imposes on an underling for violating a peer group norm, and sometimes the physical harrassment the police impose on Harlem youth rather than pressing charges for minor infractions of the law. Some members of Claude Brown's peer group felt that women deserved beatings for disobedience or so-called betrayals of one kind or another.

Aggressive acts carried out in the pursuit of gaining status or wealth or women can be identified as competitive aggression. Peer group in-fighting was most often a consequence of competition for a particular status position within the group. Aggressive acts carried out in pursuit of material goods had as targets either nonpersonal objects, such as stores or warehouses, or were personal attacks for personal belongings. Such acts of courage often won a measure of esteem from fellow peers. And, aggressive acts in competition with fellow males over women was an ongoing challenge.

Also evident in Claude Brown's story are themes of sexual aggression. A dominant example was the occupation of the pimp. His business involved the unscrupulous exploitation of women. Often there was physical coercion, and general maltreatment

135

when a pimp's woman behaved outside his control and against his wishes. Some examples of hypersexual behavior, which manifested itself in a very aggressive manner, expressed a man's insecurity with his own masculinity which drove him to overcompensate in this manner. Women who manifested a hypersexual drive were most often avoided by men. Brown's experience with one such woman challenged his intelligence in order for him to extricate himself from the relationship without losing his sense of masculine superiority. He simply withdrew-- from her and from the relationship.

Finally, we find rich examples of verbal aggression. Many different contexts of verbal aggression are expressed in Claude Brown's story. The verbal contests among the peers, commonly known as "joning" or the "dozens" were great training grounds for young boys who would develop their verbal skills to a fine art as they matured. Then there was the more serious forms of verbal insult that could also be classified as aggressive domination or authoritarian aggression or even competitive aggression, all of a nonphysical form. Verbal skills were also used in gestures of threat to opposing parties be they peer members or members of a rival gang. And then there was the general mode of speech aggressivity that reflected the harsh conditions under which these boys survived.

Another major socialization determinant was patterns of subsistence, or simply put, ways of making a living. Here we can divide up subsistence patterns into two major categories: legal and illegal. There were numerous examples of each noted in Brown's story. The legitimate occupations were those jobs of the working poor. These included the musician, waitress, bus boy, beautician, housekeeper, painter, and preacher; it also included watch repair, boxing, and military service. The illegitimate ways of making a living included drug dealing, pimping, the numbers and other forms of gambling, the murphy and other forms of conning, theft, extortion, protection, and gambling house holdups. In Brown's world, there were many more illegitimate opportunities, which were also more attractive, given his cultural environment, than there were legitimate openings to take advantage of.

The last category of socialization to note here, no less important than the others, is that of the nature and types of male-male relationships. Some of these we have already noted in other contexts. Suffice it to list them here. Most emphatically expressed were the competitive relations among peers who lived in a social system marked by dominance and hierarchy. Then there was the egalitarian intimacy a boy shared with only a few of his "brothers." There were teacher-student relationships; mentoring relationships within which a bond of mutual respect existed. This was hardly in the context of the public school, but it was evident in the reform schools that Brown attended, most importantly involving Mr. Papanek, the director, and a confidant of Brown. It was he who urged restraint and nonviolence and who established connections for Brown to go to college. Other teachers included Mrs. Meitner, the German woman who was tough but caring, also a confidant of Brown; and Mrs. Cohen, who induced Brown to read; and Stillman, the ombudsman or go-between at the school whose subtle art of diplomacy and negotiation was acknowledged by Claude Brown.

Those teachers in the school of the streets most importantly included Reno, who knew the world outside Harlem, who introduced Claude Brown to New York's downtown; Danny who taught Brown the art of stealing; and Johnny Dee who taught Brown many of the arts of survival.

Other male-male relationships included the father-son relationship full of ambivalence and strain that tended toward resolution as Brown matured. There was the hint of the grandfather-grandson relationship which briefly oriented Brown to the world of the American South. And finally there were Claude Brown's brothers; his blood brothers, his fictive brothers of his Harlem peer group, and his institutional peers who also contributed to changing the direction of his life.

137

All in all, Claude Brown's life history is enormously rich in personal and cultural detail. It is more than one boy's life growing up in Harlem; it is an ethnography of Black culture among the poor urban ghetto-dwellers. As Brown himself recognizes, there are many Claude Brown's growing up in ghettos all across the nation. Most probably, they will not be fortunate enough to find themselves in circumstances that offer them the opportunity to alter the direction in their life course. They will not meet those mentors whom they would respect and who would give them the resources for self respect. Nor will they, with any probability, find opportunities for assuming mainstream level jobs; nor will they be equipped to handle mainstream occupations. But, there are exceptions; and they will become integrated in mainstream society in one way or another.

Malcom X (1964) is one such example, whose early life in some ways paralleled that of Claude Brown. Malcom Little had very little to look forward to as a child in a small midwestern town where his teacher reminded him that, because he was a nigger, he should get those ideas of law school out of his head and settle for the status quo. Unable to accept his ascribed destiny he travelled a bit, ending up in Harlem where he became quite active and successful in illegal pursuits. While in prison, to maintain his sanity he turned to books which opened up a whole new world to him. He read voraciously. Influenced by his brother urging him to become a member of the Nation of Islam, Malcom X turned his attentions to religion, and upon entering the free society, made his mark as a brilliant leader and master of political debate.

The life history as ethnography can be a very powerful tool in the description, analysis, and understanding of a person and that culture within which that person lives. We have many examples of this dealing with Jewish ethnicity, both as true life histories and in the form of fiction, and as a result, Jewish ethnic culture may be the most written about ethnic group in America, and by that means, the most understood ethnic group for anyone who endeavors to make Jewish ethnicity a focus of study. It is an avenue open to the writers on Black ethnicity.

To date it appears that there are more Black male writers contributing in this genre that Black female writers. Because the socialization process is so important in understanding the dynamics of ethnic culture and identity there should be no reluctance for the talented to make their contribution.

VIII

SOME PRINCIPLES OF PERSONALITY FUNCTIONING

Black personality is derived from several different kinds of personality-shaping determinants. Those determinants, or categories of determinants, that are identified may vary from one discipline to another or from one writer to another depending on the perspective one favors in thinking about personality dynamics. Here I point out six general categories of personality-shaping determinants divided into two groups of three. These groups can be found schematized in the diagrams of chapters six and seven. The first group is biological in nature. I call this the infrastructure of personality because it consists of the biological "hardware" that makes personality possible and is commonly shared by members of our human species. The second group is sociocultural in nature and I identify it as the "software" consisting of the individual's adaptations to the major institutions of the ethnic group and society. It is the environment for shaping basic personality structure (Kardiner, 1945) which is that similarity of personality determined by common institutional contexts within which members of that group grow up.

The first group, the biological determinants, is called intraorganismic, i.e., internal to the individual, and can be considered a universal level of personality functioning common to our species: These categories of determinants are, specifically, neurology, age, and sex. The anatomy and neurology of the brain and spinal chord are quite similar across human populations. This extremely complex system of responsiveness and expressiveness is made up of a) our instinctual heritage of evolutionary development, b) perception, c) cognition, d) emotion, and e) behavior; all of which are highly responsive to the physical, social, and cultural environments within which the personality system must function. The determinant of age involves, on the one hand, the general process of aging from conception to death and the attendant capacities possible for that individual along the life course; and on the other hand, age is a determinant relative to how a person at any particular age is treated by those in one's social environment. The third determinant, sex, structures the direction one takes through the life course in terms of a) sex-specific instinctual drives, b) cognitive and emotional orientations, and c) role functions in the family and community.

The personality determinants of the second group are external to the individual; they function as environments in shaping individual personality. The widest field of influence is the macrostructure within which that individual lives. This normally would involve those major institutions of society that affect most all of the inhabitants. The important point to remember here is that the influence is differential relative to that group's position or status within the macrostructure. The second level of environment is the family-based structures of ethnicity. This includes all those familistic structures discussed in chapter six, but here we emphasize the extended family structure as defined by the ethnic culture. It is within this extended family context that a child learns some of the most important aspects of his or her culture that become part of the personality of that person. Such customs as patterns of discipline, respect for authority (or the lack of it), values on reciprocity and individualism, the learning of sex roles, and the like all normally occur within the context of the family, although we acknowledge that in some cases the peer group can be very influential when family members lose control over a child. These general orientations toward the various kinds of relationships are defined at least in part by the ethnic group and established through an individual's personal relationships with parent and authority figures. The lowest level of environment to consider is the individual life history; those particular situational contexts of learning and their historical successions, punctuated by developmental crises, that create in the person a concatenation of life-events that is one's life history. This is the historical environment for learning and personality development for the individual. No two life histories are the same and therefore no two individuals are ever identical.

It is the individual's life history that makes one incontrovertibly unique. It is the participation in the common institutions of ethnicity that makes those members of an ethnic group similar to each other and different from members of other ethnic groups. And, it is the macrostructure of society that allows all those within the boundaries of that society to share their nationality and hold common values regarding the integrity of that society. And finally, it is our common evolution and biology that, on the one hand, creates uniqueness in each and every human being, and on the other hand, allows all human beings the option of claiming a common membership in the "family" of humankind.

The problem, then, in arriving at some understanding of Black personality dynamics beyond the recognition of those biological and environmental forces that contribute to the shaping of Black personality, largely discussed in chapters three through six, is to employ those theoretical models of intrapsychic functioning that have particular significance in explaining how certain environmental forces shape the character of Black personality. Although there have been attempts by some Black psychologists to establish their own school of thought on the nature of Black personality (White, 1984; Jenkins, 1982; Cross, 1980; Jones, 1972; and Nobles, 1972) I feel that, because their writings do not adequately employ the knowledge and theory gained by a century of effort in the quest for the understanding of human personality and that much of the thought is Afrocentrically ideological, their efforts fall short in satisfying our needs for a deeper understanding of Black personality.

My own attempt here is to identify six models of personality dynamics that work to integrate the social, cultural and psychological levels of functioning and then to build these separate models into a deprivation-derived macro-model of Black ethnicity dynamics. In this way I keep to my original orientation to the study of Black culture, social organization, and personality by presenting general principles of human functioning against which one can understand the particular ethnic group. I call this a deprivation macro-model simply because I consider the condition of deprivation to be an important motivational force for a great deal of human activity.

143

I   II   III   IV

Deprivation --> Frustration --> Hostility --> Disposition -->
a. absolute   **to**
b. relative   **Aggression**
   (culturally
   defined)

Categories of
Deprivation:
a. possessions
b. status
c. self-worth
d. behavior
e. power
(the bases from which sex-role anxiety is derived)

Relative Deprivation: Feelings may develop when one's situation
   does not meet one's desires/expectations.

Relative Deprivation Scale:

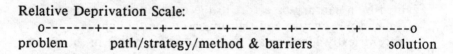

```
o-------+--------+--------+--------+--------+------o
problem        path/strategy/method & barriers        solution
```

The closer one is to the goal (solution) the higher the
motivation. The nearer the barrier to the goal the higher
the frustration and the greater the sense of deprivation
because of a) the nearness of the goal and b) the amount of
investment along the path across the barriers to the goal.

Diagram 8.1

V

Modes of Response

1. impulsivity < physical aggression / verbal aggression

2. displacement

3. involution < emotional depression / psychosomatic reaction

4. isolation < of self < emotional / psychosomatic

of group < separation / assimilation

5. denial

6. fixation

7. sublimation
   (the mechanism that facilitates achievement motivation)
   -sports
   -verbal contests
   -literature/poetry
   -law
   -medicine
   -military/police
   -social movements

145

These separate theoretical models do not stand alone, each
against the other, but rather, are dynamically related to each
other; each model pointing out areas of interdependency among
the various components of personality. They are identified as a)
the deprivation model, from which I derive the name of this
macro-model complex, b) the elements of power model, c) the
sex-role anxiety model, d) the achievement motivation model, e)
the frustration-aggression model, and f) the revitalization model.

The Deprivation Macro-Model

A basic postulate of this model is that all human beings are
born with basic needs which must be satisfied in order that
survival and development take place (Maslow, 1954; Erikson,
1963). The more completely these human needs are satisfied the
greater are the possibilities for actualizing human potential. This
list of basic needs is suggestive, but not exhaustive. They
include food (and here I refer to the nature of nutrition a
mother-to-be lives on prior to the conception of her child and
through that child's gestation, since the condition of her body
and what she ingests through pregnancy means a great deal to
that developing child), shelter, protection, possessions,
communication, identity, status, self-worth, and power. The
extent and manner of satisfying these needs is relative to the
natural environment, age, and culture of the individual; and most
probably relative to the innate need-dispositions of any particular
individual. An adjunct postulate is that a completely satisfied
need is no longer a motivator of behavior. Therefore, a
necessary condition of motivation is the incomplete satisfaction
of a need, be it basic or relative and learned. This postulate
may appear to be a contradiction to the first, which states that
proper growth and development depends upon the satisfaction and
fulfillment of human needs. But, here the resolution rests with
the recognition that the fulfillment of one level of human needs
makes it possible to embark upon the satisfaction of another
level of human needs. This process is known as growth and
development; or, in a word, maturity, that stage toward which a
healthy person strives to actualize.

I conceive the phenomenon of <u>deprivation</u> as a first cause in a whole series and configuration of responsive behaviors, some of which are found among all warm-blooded animals, such as frustration and aggression, and some of which are uniquely human responses. In the category of deprivation I recognize two forms: a) <u>absolute deprivation</u>, which is required for survival and normal growth and development of body, mind, and sociality; and b) <u>relative deprivation</u>, which is learned, and most often culturally defined, and has more to do with one's expectations relative to one's actual situation (Aberle, 1962). Normally, relative needs, and hence, relative deprivations, are outgrowths and elaborations of the absolute or basic needs and deprivations.

Absolute or Basic Needs and Deprivations

Although many basic needs are self-evident, such as food, shelter and protection, I wish to elaborate on two such needs that are important in our appreciation of the dynamics of Black ethnicity, viz., power and identity, and, with regard to the latter, more particularly, sex-role identity.

The Power Model

Power is a very common concept with a highly generalized application. Here, of course we are talking about power through symbolic communication more than about mechanical power. I would define power as <u>the ability to produce intended effects</u>. And I would further elaborate this simple definition by adding the Weberian notion that the acquisition and maintenance of power is often proportionate to one's <u>control of the resources upon which others depend</u> (Weber, 1947). Power must be conceived not just in terms of personal persuasion, political influence, masculine domination or even spiritual power, but must be conceived in the widest context which also includes the more subtle uses of power such as a child's ability to influence a peer in some way or a woman's ability to influence her man, or an individual's ability to alter his or her way of thinking and feeling about their world (McClelland, 1975). In this way we see a human being who is powerless at birth gradually gain developmental skills that, stage after stage, increase that person's ability to act upon the world. In this way we see that the sense

147

of power is critical to the formation of the self and to the formation of ethnic group identity. The range of human power can be seen in such small events as a child's persuasion of the parent to purchase candy while in the supermarket to a charismatic leader building a great social movement with a following of millions.

It is not only important to appreciate the fact that power is a vital element in the development of an individual human being and in the identity of the ethnic group, but also to understand the bases from which one may acquire power (Kahn, 1984). These bases or sources of power become the very nature and expression of the power wielded.

The first type of power we can call coercive power. Coercive power is commonly recognized as the ability to force others to one's will by threat of physical violence; but it also includes the ability to deliver punishments, levy fines, effect demotions, and persuade through the expression of disapproval.

A second basis of power is through reward. One may exercise power through reward by accessing and contributing resources that are valued by the recipient. These resources are usually known in terms of money, food, promotion, and affection.

A third basis of power is called referent power. In this case one exerts power over or influence of another through one's ability to have the other value the qualities of the powerholder. The other identifies with the powerholder and wants to be like the powerholder and so allows one's self to be shaped by the powerholder. This form of power is most commonly found in the parent-child relationship, where the child finds the avenue to power through the incorporation of those qualities of the parent that the child perceives and powerful. The charismatic leader is another example of referent power in a larger context, where the leader becomes something of a father-figure or mother-figure or savior who can deliver his people from a certain difficulty.

148

A fourth basis of power is called expert power. This includes having superior skills that others value. These skills can be almost anything that a population finds useful in a person and can be simple mechanical skills of strength or accuracy in performing certain tasks or may be skills borne of an uncommon fund and application of knowledge.

A fifth basis of power is information. One gains this power though the ability to acquire valued information that is recognized as knowledge, and at the higher levels, is appreciated as wisdom. Possession of this information allows one to influence and change the behavior of those who value this information. Of course, education is the most systematic form of the use of knowledge whether it be informal as with the parental use of knowledge with their children or formal as with the teacher's education of their students. One's ability to disclose information that has material, emotional, or spiritual value is of very high priority and stresses the value of quality education for those who wish to improve their quality of life. We must also recognize another aspect of information power, especially in the age of the computer, and that is the ability to access information about others that gives that person or group a certain power over the person who is the referent of the information. For example, the IRS may access information about a person who is found to owe a great deal of back taxes. This empowers the IRS to press charges against this person and to levy fines against this person and even imprison him.

The sixth and last basis of power to note here is legitimate power. Legitimate power refers to the means by which one gains the right to influence and persuade others to comply. Legitimate power rests, most often, on the consensus of the group as to the proper paths to access power, whether it be by election, by appointment, by divine inspiration, or by being the successor in the blood line designated to perform a certain role in society. Legitimate power is wielded by one who is recognized as an authority. Authority, by its very definition, implies the accessing of power through a legitimate means. It has its greatest significance in the context of political organization which is built

149

up from five elements: a) some form of personal power, b) authority, c) legitimacy, d) control over the delivering of both positive and negative social sanctions, i.e., rewards and punishments, and e) an orientation to some territorial boundary.

These six bases of power that Kahn cites (1984) are not mutually exclusive, but rather overlap in themselves to one extent or another and can be possessed singly, but more commonly are possessed as a whole by an individual to one extent or another. That is, any particular person usually has access to varying degrees of all six of these forms of power. All human beings have the basic need to possess and express a minimum of these forms of power and a great proportion of persons go on to develop one or more of these bases of power relative to their personal goals and cultural standards, and environmental constraints.

The Sex-Role Identity Model
The second absolute or basic need I will note here, which if one is kept from satisfying becomes an absolute or basic deprivation, is sex-role identity. The incomplete or partial deprivation of this form of identity generates what we now recognize as sex-role anxiety. The theory of sex-role anxiety has important significance for Black Americans and affects the sexes differentially in that males appear to be far more affected than their female counterparts.

This theory is tied very closely to the matrifocal form of social organization. The postulate is that a child incorporates important aspects of its sex-role identity at a very early period, from about ages one and a half through six. The thesis is that a boy who grows up in a matrifocal household without an enduring relationship to a man with whom that young boy can identify with will consequently identify with his mother, i.e., take on many personality traits of the woman who is his mother, and subsequently, when maleness or masculinity becomes a meaningful mode of identity, around the age of preadolescence, he will experience an anxiety borne of his cross-sex identity, and to compensate, will overemphasize his masculine role in order to

150

convince himself and others that he is not lacking in those traits which define his male role and identity in society. This overcompensation takes the form of the machismo complex consisting of high levels of aggressivity, predisposition to violent behavior, an orientation to dominance, especially the dominance of women, and particular skills in the manipulation of others.

In considering this behavior complex we must be able to distinguish between ethnicity and class. For this pattern or configuration of behavior is often identified with the male lower class where one can find a preponderance of single-parent families. However, if Black Americans remain largely among the lower socioeconomic class of American society this theory will hold since the socioeconomic forces influence the expression of ethnicity. However, one must also recognize that this pattern of single-parent households is no more restricted to the lower socioeconomic class of U.S. society, but rather has spread to the middle classes which are also affected by economic stress, rapid social change, and an increasing divorce rate at least in part caused by anomic conditions of American culture.

This issue arose out of a concern for the causes of juvenile delinquency and streetcorner gangs (Miller, 1958). It was argued by Miller that this concern with toughness, smartness, physical prowess, the defiance of danger, and rebellion against the law was a reaction to the more feminine traits of compliance, passivity, dependence, and gullibility. In psychoanalytic parlance this behavior orientation pattern was a reaction- formation; the disposition to act out a pattern of behavior that is the opposite of the original impulse. In this case it was a reaction-formation to the learned cross-sex identity. The reaction-formation is an unconsciously operating personality ego-defense mechanism that functions to defend the ego against painful and unacceptable impulses and experiences.

Studies which have focused upon the Black community have found the sex-role anxiety thesis helpful in understanding the nature of gang behavior and delinquency. Davis and Dollard (1940) and Rohrer and Edmonson (1960) made intensive studies

151

of New Orleans youth--the latter being a follow-up study of the former. They found a largely "matriarchal" situation within which these youth were being socialized. They interpreted the function of the gang as an all-important socialization group which helped its members separate from their female identity figures and demonstrate their autonomy from those traits recognized as feminine. Rohrer and Edmonson emphasized that the gang had the critical function of replacing the absent father with a group which had its own authority structure and from which a boy could rebuild his masculine identity. The socialization process was severe and included fighting to establish one's place in a pecking order, hazing of those who fell short of the often hypermasculine ideals, verbal aggression in maintaining one's status in the group and one's personal integrity, and a severe enforcement of conformity to gang standards and norms. This study of New Orleans youth hardly differs from what Claude Brown has written about his Harlem.

Beatrice Whiting's study (1965) further demonstrates that cross-sex identification in boys creates a predisposition to aggressivity and physical violence and that this pattern is most strongly seen when that boy emerges into an adult world dominated by men. The sociocultural factor is very important here because where the cultural ideals and social pressures to act in a distinctively masculine way are not highly emphasized, or where the definition of masculinity is not given in terms of dominance, aggressivity, and prowess, the male has less pressure to change his identity if it was originally formed out of a feminine model, and therefore, motivationally and culturally, there would not be the anxiety to act out a hypermasculine role.

A developmental problem occurs in an individual, who as a child experienced certain kinds of trauma, pressures to achieve goals and perform roles that were unrealizable. As long as a child experiences the successful achievement of learned roles and accomplished goals, normal development and maturation can occur. But, where trauma is experienced fixation punctuates the developmental course by retarding growth in one or more aspects of the personality. This is no more evident than at the adolescent stage when the child, on the threshhold of adulthood, strives to become the image of the person inculcated in them. For boys, most importantly, the image of masculinity becomes fixated at the adolescent level because both internal blocks, in the form of anxieties and fears, and external blocks, barriers to the achievement of successful adult male roles, results in what psychologists recognize as identity foreclosure (Hauser, 1971). Blocks to the further maturation of the male sex-role result in the common complaint of women that their men are still acting in adolescent ways. This intuitive insight is right on the mark because the grown man has failed to change his self-image and role performance and so continues to engage in the games of bravado, domination, self-oriented pursuits that are normal for adolescents and frustrating for the women who love these men.

I would like to conclude this section by noting that this interpretation of Black masculine behavior falls short if it does not recognize that hypermasculine behavior is motivated by anger; anger against the impulses of the incorporated female that threaten that male's identity as a man; anger against the absent father who was not there as a consistent and enduring model; and anger against the society whose rules and norms perpetuate a pattern of oppression which prevents many a Black boy's father from achieving anything a young boy can be proud of. Yet, if we can learn anything from the Virginia Heyer Young study (chapter 7), it is that the mother has a lot to do with a young boy's actualization of his masculinity through his learning how to maintain autonomy, his mood sensitivity training, and the learning of strategies of manipulation as well as learning the strategies for living in a bicultural world that Black children must adapt to.

One last point must be noted before considering the next theoretical model and that is that even absolute or basic needs or their deprivations have the element of relativity in

them. For example, there is no question that without food
and water we die. But, we also recognize that we are
assuming a minimum amount of food and water to forestall
dying. This absolute minimum amount will vary from one
individual to another, depending on their size and weight, the
quantity of fat and water already in their body, and
metabolism rate. Therefore, this absolute need is relative to
the above-stated conditions. Power and sex-role identity are
similar in that there must be a certain "critical mass," so-to-
speak, in order for that individual to maintain normal adaptive
living routines. But, power and sex-role identity are also
relative to the conditions in their environment, viz.,
sociocultural conditions. Therefore, these basic needs, or
their deprivations, are relative to the social arrangements one
is involved in, i.e., the social environment, and the values and
meaning given to particular situations and behaviors, i.e., the
cultural environment. Thus, for example, among Jews, the
definition of masculinity emphasizes family responsibility, so a
nonaggressive person does not suffer any stigma. But, in
Claude Brown's Harlem a nonaggressive person would suffer a
good deal of stigma.

The Relative Deprivation Model

Relative deprivation refers to one's actual situation not
meeting the ideals, standards, or expectations one has formed
with regard to material, psychological, economic, political, or
spiritual concerns. Relative deprivation is usually culturally
defined in terms of the standards, ideals, and expectations
that are learned by the members of a population. It is always
relative either with regard to what someone else has or is or
with regard to what some other group has or is. It very
often involves the elaboration of basic needs that were noted
above, but may involve just about anything one can imagine
that one wishes for but as yet does not have. Aberle (1962)
is very specific about those categories involved in deprivation:
possessions, status, self-worth, behavior. I have added the
overarching category of power which is elaborated above and
include those basic needs of any person or group that stand
to be deprived. The major point to note here is that one

does not have to be deprived of a basic or absolute need to feel deprived. One may, in fact, lead a very comfortable life and still feel deprived, say in terms of a man's annual salary, because his neighbor, doing just about the same job makes considerably more. Or, to use another example at the group level, one group, which is the object of widespread discrimination in the larger society, sees members of another group enjoying much greater freedom to go where they want to go, acquire resources they desire such as jobs and money, or having rights and privileges that exclude members of the discriminated class.

We can say then that basic need deprivation certainly contributes to one's sense of frustration, but it appears that a stronger sense of frustration is experienced when one's situation falls short of the expectation of what one desires. As our continuum model illustrates, if an individual acknowledges a problem or an undesirable state of affairs, there is normally an attempt made at formulating a solution, no matter what the scale of the problem is. The solution involves a path from the problem to the solution. This path is the method, the strategy, for overcoming the problem. Now, along this path is situated a set of barriers. Some of these barriers are foreseeable and predictable and others are not. Progress along this path involves an investment of energy and this in turn builds motivation to accomplish the goal. Normally, the less energy invested in the solution the less motivation there is. Therefore, the closer the barrier is to the problem, the less energy has so far been invested, the less motivation there will be to continue. In other words, the frustration level is less, proportionate to the investment given. Therefore, we may state that the closer one is to the goal the higher the motivation. And, the nearer the barrier is to the goal the higher the frustration, and hence, the greater the sense of deprivation; deprivation not only in terms of the original problem, but also in terms of the investment already given. A small scale example and a large scale example will illustrate this. A student who flunks out of college in his or her freshman year has given relatively little investment.

155

Motivation may have been less than one's expectations, but the barriers to continuing on precluded any elaborate goals deriving from acquiring the diploma. On the other hand, if this student works their way through almost four years of college and a barrier arises in their senior year that prevents the student from graduating, the motivation is great and the frustration will be high and there will be a great sense of deprivation relative to one's expectations of what one might have become if graduation could be achieved. The second example is the Watts riots of 1968. Watts, a suburb of Los Angeles, was not a community stricken with abject poverty. The standards of living were in fact quite middle class although the Black members of that community still struggled to maintain their quality of life. They were almost there but not quite. One antagonizing reminder of that was the way representatives of the power structure, the police, treated these people, viz., as second class citizens. The stresses and pressures and frustrations of everyday life built up that summer. Whatever safety valves were operating previously, failed in the face of a police harrassment of a community member, and the community went up in flames. Many so-called experts were completely surprised by the riot, but hindsight and a useful theory took account of the incident.

The Achievement Motivation Model

Relative deprivation does not necessarily result in negative consequences. Relative deprivation is often the motivating force for an individual or a group achieving uncommonly difficult goals. The achievement motive has been researched since the early 1950's (McClelland, et. al., 1953). From that research we can derive information that allows an individual or a group as a whole to evaluate the nature and strength of their levels of motivation to achieve. In our analysis of Black culture, social organization, and personality we may find those aspects that can be set against our theoretical formulation in order to evaluate the nature and extent of Black achievement motivation.

156

The achievement motive may be defined as the disposition to strive toward a kind of satisfaction which is derived from one's successful attainment of a goal in competition with others in terms of some standard of excellence that exists beyond the realm of mediocrity. This definition of achievement motivation raises four major questions: 1) What are the implications and consequences for an individual, for an ethnic group, in possessing this form of motivation? 2) What are the personality characteristics, the configuration of important personality traits, that are typical of one possessing achievement motivation? 3) What is the social organization of the family like and what is the nature of the socialization process that inculcates this form of motivation? 4) What are the significant features of society that allow this form of motivation to be expressed and actualized?

The answer to the first question is rather obvious. Those persons who possess this form of energy are going to strive toward something greater than what they have or what they are. If enough members of the ethnic group possess similar qualities the sum of the individual efforts will have unmistakable consequences for the group as a whole, provided that the barriers to success that have been erected by the larger society can be surmounted.

The personality traits found to be significant in the mobilization of achievement motivation were found over and over again. They included eight key personality attributes: 1) a willingness to take moderate risks; 2) a rather consistent stream of energetic innovative activity; 3) a willingness to take personal responsibility for one's actions and for the consequences of one's actions; 4) a searching for and application of knowledge gained from the results of one's actions; 5) a fairly consistent willingness to postpone immediate rewards in favor of greater future rewards (this is usually learned from a very young age by seeing their parents making sacrifices in order to give their children their best chance, thereby hoping that the success of their child will raise the whole family up); 6) a greater-than-normal ability to recall failures and remember tasks not yet completed; 7) a future time perspective; and 8) an awareness of and an interest in situations involving an element of personal control and the avoidance of becoming invested in situations that involve pure chance. This then is the personality design for achievement and success. It provides a gauge for one's own assessment of his or her personal or ethnic group possibilities. One can turn these eight points into their opposites to see clearly what type of personality stands to get nowhere but the status quo situation.

The nature of the social relationships within the family group and the attendant pattern of socialization appears clearly as that configuration generating a high motivation in the children to achieve. Six features of the primary group stand out: 1) From an early age families reward their children for acts of achievement; 2) independence and self-reliance is stressed, even in very young children; 3) a high value is placed on education as an important avenue of social mobility; 4) within the sanctum of the home we find a rather dominant mother and a passive, somewhat remote father; 5) it is a highly democratic family structure where the children have considerable influence in family affairs and a great deal of opportunity to practice assertiveness; 6) the mode of discipline is symbolic, rather than applying corporal punishment, and is based upon instilling guilt for not behaving as the parents, especially the mother, expects the child to behave, i.e., it is based on the threat of the withdrawal of love, especially maternal love, that is otherwise lavished upon the child for "good" behavior.

No matter how strong the motivation to achieve, the society must be structured in such a way as to allow some energy to be expressed. To the extent that it sets up barriers against the achievement of higher goals, frustration, anger, and general discontent will be experienced by the individual and by the group as a whole if that form of motivation is prominently generated by the ethnic culture. The society that provides and maintains appropriate rewards for the achievement of higher goals, be they in the form of material wealth, social status, or political position, allows highly motivated individuals to succeed. The free enterprise system is a powerful encouragement for achievement and it must be maintained and defended if need be against social forces that would discourage individual effort.

This, then, is what the system of achievement motivation looks like. I have placed this system within the context of relative deprivation because the motivation comes from a need not satisfied, viz., the higher goals not yet attained. The sense of relative deprivation is also felt in response to the realistic or imagined barriers that one must overcome in order to fulfill a particular set of expectations and achieve a particular stage of personal maturation. If one compares general patterns of Black culture to this achievement model we find a less-than-clear-cut picture. But that is the nature of complex human reality. We certainly do find important elements of achievement motivation as well as the barriers in society that frustrate the actualization of that achievement, and a good deal of anger that is generated as a response to the frustrations of those social barriers. There is one element of Black culture that I believe figures importantly into the picture of Black achievement motivation which is not emphasized in the literature. I find a great deal of motivation to strive and to struggle, sometimes against overwhelming odds, among members of the Black community in both the lower as well as the middle socioeconomic classes. Although this high degree of motivation lacks the structural configuration of high achievement motivation, Blacks forced to survive the day-to-day end up <u>behaving</u> in ways that are similar to the end-product of the motivational model. We must, then, contribute this additional factor, the necessity for survival, to the general conclusions of achievement research.

The Frustration-Aggression Model

We now come to the next stage of our macro-model of personality dynamics, the frustration-aggression process. I have stated that deprivation, in its two forms, is a first cause for the generation of the experience of frustration and consequent emotional states. This is a lawful process: Deprivation generates frustration which, in turn, generates the emotional experience of hostility, and hostility generates the disposition to aggression. This has come to be a postulate of modern behavioral science.

The question of how particular animals and animal species express this process has been thoroughly researched. For the rat species and for the human species there is a voluminous literature. However, systematic comparison of patterns of expression of anger and dispositions to aggression among various ethnic groups is not well researched. Fortunately, at least one Black psychologist (Wilson, 1978) has given serious attention to the psychosocial dynamics of his people through the perspective that is somewhat akin to the frustration-aggression model I am elaborating here. He is especially sensitive to the deprivations of his people; their barriers and consequent frustrations, their hostility and anger, and, what is especially important for us here, their consequent dispositions to particular patterns of behavior.

Wilson has very strong feelings about the physical barriers to quality of life that exist in the ghetto environment; barriers at this level that preclude one from barely getting started in changing their existential situation.

> ...garbage-filled streets, run-down and shuttered stores and burnt-out and abandoned cars and buildings, crumbling apartment houses, deteriorating real estate, rats, roaches, flies, stale smells....overcrowdedness on the streets and in the apartments, the lack of heat and hot warter [sic]....lack of basic physical services and upkeep, the general decay of all things physical... the abundance of all that is rottening [sic], decaying, overused, overcrowded, outmoded, and a sparsity of all that is needed, but unavailable; the over-abundance of health-damaging conditions and the absence of wholesome, preventative conditions. The over-abundance of life destroying instruments, objects and

establishments and absence of life-supporting instruments, objects and establishments; shelters that don't protect from the ravages of the elements, men and vermin, infestation and disease; physical environments that provide no vistas and scenes that uplift the spirit, but which amply provide a mind-deadening drabness, sameness and unrelieved pictures of poverty and squalor....This...shapes the minds of the inhabitants, forces them to narrow their perspectives, to concentrate on adapting and surviving in those conditions, spends their cognitive talents on the trivialities of a highly fragmented environment and this forces them to take their pleasures where and when they find them, to take them immediately and to constantly seek escape--most by...alcohol, drugs, chronic sexual involvement, to take from their fellow members through crime, whatever amount of scarce resources they may happen to possess (p. 202).
In the garbage-filled streets roam pregnant teenage girls, dirty, unattended children, prostitutes, pimps, hustlers, muggers, con men, homosexuals. Noise and loud rock music rend the air, the stench of decaying buildings, of the smell of urine wafts out onto the streets from darkened hallways where may be lurking dangers of all types. What businesses there are are petty and exploitive, their dusty merchandise peering out from window gates. Others have long departed the neighborhood and left behind a legacy of boarded-up windows or burnt-out shells of buildings. Bars, pool halls, "clubs," dry cleaners and storefront churches and candy stores, that are in reality numbers joints, share the sidewalks (p. 204).

We must keep in mind that this view is but one person's statement, although it is the statement of a sensitive Black psychologist who appreciates how this type of physical environment creates a sea of frustration for its inhabitants.

161

Wilson cites the economic frustrations, which are
commonly known, including unemployment and
underemployment, which he says are worse today than it was
at the height of the Great Depression (p. 203). Basic
economic goods and services are difficult to obtain due to the
scarcity of dollars accessible to the inhabitants of the ghetto.
Social service agencies normally attempt to allocate critical
goods and services to the needy, but this is often done
unevenly and in quantities too meager to be of value to the
recipients. The poverty is further antagonized by the
shoddiness of merchandise, higher-than-average prices, and the
gouging tactics of merchants and landlords (Ibid.). The
economics of poverty is further complicated by the continuous
outflow of capital, lack of investment by business or city
groups, and little extension of credit. Food stamps and ADC
and menial work that barely allows one to make a living only
encourages one to take advantage of opportunities to become
involved in illegitimate means of making a living. Illegal
economic pursuits including outright criminality are both a
consequence and a cause of the cycle of poverty found in the
ghetto ecology. It is an ecology and an economy that is
marked by ubiquitous frustration and grinding tedium where
one lives day to day.

Wilson also discusses the psychosocial barriers to the
elevation of quality of life; barriers to the actualization of the
goals of achievement. It is a socialization perspective that is
used, the point being that children exposed to the world of
the ghetto streets can learn no model of how to succeed in
the larger world--the white-dominated world. To the average
child of the ghetto the situations experienced and the adult
role-models available to learn from only ensure one's place in
the status quo. Wilson's image of idle men either gambling,
wolfing after women, ever after the sexual conquest, or
involved in some act of physical violence, gives no child, male
or female, a very good image of worthiness, and creates
confusion as the child grows up and sees other ways of being-
in-the-world, especially the middle class modes of life. And
for the boys there is staying out of school, sidewalk sports,

aimless wandering, and seeking after thrills to break the monotony of their lives (Ibid.).

Frustrations are further intensified by one's sense of curtailed freedom in the community. As Wilson puts it,

> The prevailing [psychosocial] atmosphere is one of fear--sometimes conscious, sometimes unconscious. Fear of being mugged, assaulted, insulted, witnessing revolting acts and events or of returning to a robbed apartment are prevalent. Chronic tension and anxiety force the inhabitants to be constantly hyperalert-- even inside their homes or asleep in bed. The attitudes of distrust and suspicion are the best defensive ones for the ghetto dweller. Consequently, paranoia is a way of life and edgedness a chronic state of being. The police are the colonial military whose main function seems to be that of bullying and oppressing the local populace and protecting rent-gouging landlords' properties and the properties of absentee, exploitive businessmen. Thus the individual ghetto member feels unprotected and deserted by the government (Ibid., p. 205).

Wilson continues to elaborate this emotional climate which is generated by enduring deprivations and unrelieved frustrations:

> The constant threat of violence and intimidation wraps the community in a heavy, oppressive cloud. The attitudes of unfathomable discontent, undirected, unrelieved hostility, or a constant desire to escape are shared by everyone. A constant state of readiness for confrontation, to flee from it, or to avoid it. For undefinable mixed feelings expressed in unpredictable ways connects all the inhabitants of the ghetto, friend and foe...and stranger alike (Ibid.).

Wilson characterizes the emotional climate of politics in the ghetto as one of apathy, a consequence of political

163

disorganization and a sense of powerlessness. Combined with
a lack of political self-assertiveness ghetto inhabitants look to
escapism for relief, which of course does not confront the
problems but rather hides from them. The escapism takes the
forms of physical aggression, habitual use of alcohol and other
powerful drugs, sexual preoccupations, and "emotional religious
meetings" (Ibid.).

Although Wilson's picture of Black ghetto life is bleak,
one also derives a sense of intense life experience. One sign
of this can be read from the complex variety of life
experiences and lifestyles that Wilson alludes to (without
giving it much positive credit). The ghetto life is full of
contradictions, or at least, opposing and noncomplementary
modes of living. One must extrapolate from this that a child
or a youth or an adult who begins to reflect on his or her
life-situation is forced to make some choices about which path
to follow. One must use the resources of self-reliance and
the guidance of peers, family or church to weigh one's
chances along one path or another. One must decide where
the greater rewards lie. It is clear that young women often
make decidedly different life-course choices than the men; and
that this is largely due to sex differences and the differential
socioeconomic pressures that bear on men as opposed to
women.

In sum, within the physical, socioeconomic, and
psychological environments of an individual living in the
ghetto a variety of deprivations, barriers, and frustrations
exist that block the paths to one's betterment of life
circumstances. These deprivations, barriers and frustrations
are self-evident of the building of hostility and anger, an
emotional climate that easily predisposes all but the most stoic
and religious to acts of aggression in one form or another.
And Wilson gives strong and expressive testament to this. But
human beings are very complex animals. We are intelligent,
creative, and highly social animals. And if the expression of
direct physical aggression were the only means at our
disposal, we would have extinguished ourselves long ago. In

fact, we have many modalities for expressing potentially destructive impulses at our disposal. The last stage of my macro-model delineates a number of these modes of human expression.

Modes of Response

We have been discussing a chain of psychosocial causation: deprivation-->frustration-->hostility-->disposition to aggression-->modes of response. This process has very complex interrelations, the extent of which can only be sketched here. But, it is important to know that these categories in our macro-model reflect thought, sentiment, and behavior that are in a feedback process. That means that some of the reactions that we shall discuss in the modes of response category were also involved in the causal process at an earlier stage. For example, as Wilson has stated, much of the street behavior is a response to the economic privations and political powerlessness experienced, especially by ghetto-dwellers, as a result of the racist culture and power structure of America. Escapism is also a mode of response, a reaction, a consequence, to what is individually experienced as overwhelming odds against one's chances for anything better in life. But, the patterns of street behavior and modes of escapism are also causes for certain consequences that occur later. To cite just one example, one that Wilson feels strongly about, these patterns provide little for a child to model him- or herself after, and hence, create, or cause, a vicious cycle of identity foreclosure, poverty and powerlessness. My own opinion here, given this example, is that the males of ghetto society are more in jeopardy than the females, the latter of whom are more involved in family life and have a greater grounding in the meaning of life, viz., the bearing and rearing of children in a familistic social network.

My own categories of modes of response follow a psychoanalytic conceptualization. Therefore, these categories are first headed by a psychoanalytic concept under which a specific set of behaviors are listed as examples. I have two general objectives here, which are no less relevant for what I write throughout in the book, and that is to a) foster a sense of understanding about the issues discussed, and b) to make visible certain destructive, i.e., maladaptive, tendencies that are caused by a deprivation process so that individuals and groups alike can apply their insights, energies, and ingenuity for positive change; especially since my last response mode is, in fact, a positive mechanism for successful adaptation.

1. Impulsivity. The most primitive, simplest, reaction to the deprivation-frustration-hostility process is direct aggression. It is a spontaneous and impulsive act directed at the source of the frustration. It is often interpreted by the aggressor as retaliation. The means and degree of aggressive act will be determined by the context, i.e., who is involved, where and when the situation takes place, and the means of aggression at one's disposal. Impulsive aggression may be either physical aggression involving fists and/or weapons, or, it may take the form of verbal aggression, which here includes insult. In either case the intent is to do harm against the perceived source of frustration. Many psychologists, including Wilson, make a distinction in the scale of the source of frustration. First there is the micro-level scale where interpersonal conflict is perceived as the critical matter. But, the professionals see the problem on a macro-level, a much broader-based scale, where the source of the frustration is really the nature of the macro-structure of society. From this point of view, they would say, and I would agree, that the aggression expressed is a function of displacement.

2. Displacement. Displacement is the process whereby the person cannot retaliate directly against the source of the deprivation and frustration and yet the energy of the anger must be relieved. Therefore, one finds a target that appears to be appropriate and controllable. For example, a man working on the job is censured in front of his workmates by the boss for not doing a good enough job. The censure includes some elements of insult which is humiliating to the worker and enrages him. But he wants to keep his job and so

does not retaliate and takes the censure quietly.
Nevertheless, the boss has challenged his sense of masculinity,
has situationally deprived him of it because the man
experiences the episode as an emasculation. The frustration is
great because he would have liked to kill the boss, yet did
nothing. He comes home after a long and difficult day all
bottled up and is met by his wife who greets him with a
nagging litany of how he didn't leave money for the children's
lunch, didn't take out the garbage when he left for work,
failed to call her at lunch-time, and what did he do with the
fifty dollars of his paycheck he said he was going to give her.
This is a critical point when the bomb can easily go off.

3. Involution. Black culture maintains a rich inventory of
expressivity. Black Americans are rather spontaneous in
expressing their impulse life in the appropriate contexts,
usually within the primary group or among peers. That is why
there is a greater emphasis of verbal and physical expression
than we might find among the Anglo-Saxon or Slavic groups,
for example. But, in response to deprivation and frustration
we find that involution does occur among Black Americans and
it must be dealt with.

The concept of involution refers to a process of turning
the anger inward. This turning inward can be seen on two
levels: turning anger against the self or turning anger against
one's own group when the prevailing source of deprivation lies
outside the group. Turning the anger against the self can be
emotional or physical. When one goes the emotional route it
is commonly recognized as depression. Where one finds no
target to vent anger and no sufficient mechanism to dissipate
it, such as an emotional religious service, one may bottle up
the anger and allow it to "eat" one up. This is usually
experienced as being slowed down, with periods of sadness,
insomnia, inability to think quickly and accurately, lack of
sexual vitality, thoughts of suicide, and may include any
number of physical (psychosomatic) ailments. If the involution
is physical we find the individual involved in self-destructive
acts. These acts take the form of driving recklessly,

ingesting dangerous chemical substances, precipitating arguments or conflicts with people that can do serious harm, or engaging in serious criminal activities, especially when the payoff is not that great.

But, involution may also be perceived as being turned against the group. Again, this is the perspective of many sociologists and psychologists who are sensitive to the macro-structural deprivations that turn a people against each other. Probably the strongest example of this level of involution is gang behavior. This can be seen on both the levels of intragang and intergang behavior. In both cases the levels of aggression are high. Physical combat is virtually a daily experience within the gang and intergang combat is carried out regularly, either as a retaliation for some offense or as a ritual act of masculinity. Serious physical injury and homicide is common. To the social scientist the anger has been displaced and the aggression involuted because the real targets, the original sources of deprivation and frustration lay beyond their reach.

4. Isolation. In the strict psychoanalytic sense isolation refers to the isolation of the emotional significance of a traumatic event from that very event. That is, the individual may be very much aware of a traumatic event or ongoing painful set of circumstances but will isolate that event from its emotional significance. In the Black social environment of resource deprivation, a common reaction is one of apathy. A sense of indifference may be an adaptive response to a set of circumstances one cannot control. Wilson also makes the point that apathy may be expected when one has no means of dealing with an enduring frustration and where one feels that any action against the source of the frustration will be met with severe punishment (p. 210). The attitude or sentiment can be illustrated as, "I know its there, but it doesn't bother me. Besides, nothin' I can do about it." The social manifestation is one of withdrawal from actions against the frustrating circumstances and/or isolation from those who are either the source of the frustration or from those whose

168

concerted and organized activity could pose a threat to the people responsible for those deprivations.

5. Denial. The refusal to acknowledge events which are painful in themselves or which produce painful consequences is called denial. Most relevant example here would be the denial of the race problem. From this issues a denial of the existence of the mean-spirited barriers to the betterment of one's quality of life. And further, one is then issuing denials of the painful experiences that arise from those originally denied events and circumstances. It is certainly one motivational force for what some psychologists call the "flight into reality" which refers to the pursuing of activities and intense experiences that crowd out those painful feelings. Activities which serve this purpose well include gambling, preoccupation with and intense pursuit of sexual involvements, male adolescent pursuits such as "gang business" which includes domination in establishing and maintaining one's place in the peer (gang) group and aggression against real and imagined threats to one's integrity.

Both isolation and denial motivate and predispose one to flights of fantasy and magical thinking. This refers to the propensity for one to imagine or believe that the path to gaining or acquiring something valued is realizable when it isn't, or when one elaborates an idea or situation which is known not to be true but is elaborated anyhow because it raises the status or image of the storyteller. The literature strongly suggests that it is the males who are more prone to this activity (Liebow, Hannerz, Wilson). This may be because there is a greater social pressure on Black males to access symbols of status and power and yet these very symbols may be inaccessible; and so "myth-making," as Hannerz puts it, may become prevalent in order to compensate for the painful experience of deprivation one feels about those resources that define his sex-role identity. This process very likely contributes to what Wilson terms stereotypy. That is the dispostion to act in a manner that fits a preconceived image held by a significant number of people who are deemed

169

important in that person's life. For males this might easily be recognized as "Black macho" (Staples, 1982). Hardly different from the standard American macho image, it normally involves a greater elaboration of hypermasculinity than what might be found in the white world. The price one pays is in the expression of one's own individuality and one's self-knowledge both of which are sacrificed on the altars of peer pressure and image-making.

6. Reaction-formation. This mechanism defends against an unacceptable impulse by creating in the individual an experience of its opposite. To continue our example of machismo as an element of Black masculinity, we can hypothesize that if an individual has learned a cross-sex identity, and as a male, is experiencing sex-role anxiety, he will compensate for this by engaging in role-behavior that is unquestionably masculine, i.e., hypermasculine. And, if he is in any way successful in this role-playing activity, he will not only convince himself but, also will convince his peers of his manliness. But, the feeling of effeminate disposition can remain for many years even after a man has met the cultural standards of his society.

7. Fixation. Failure of continued growth and development of one or more aspects of the personality is termed fixation in psychoanalytic parlance. This may occur at any stage of the maturation process, but has its highest frequency in childhood. It may be an intrapersonal occurrance as when an individual experiences a traumatic situation or pattern of situations, such as harsh discipline, and has great difficulty in growing beyond that period when this discipline was invoked. Or, it may occur on a social level where there just aren't any models available to learn higher levels of thinking and behavior. An example of this can be found in the identity-foreclosure phenomenon where an adolescent male often has no adult models to learn higher levels of maturity. The boy is fully dependent upon his peer group to learn the appropriate sex-role. If the only model for adult behavior is the peer group, or adults who have not gotten beyond the

170

adolescent level of maturation, the emotional development of that boy's identity will be foreclosed at that stage. It cannot be emphasized too much that it is the emotional level of development that is salient here; that has a great deal to do with the direction of the cognitive and behavioral growth, for it is the emotional predisposition that lies at the foundation of motivation and direction of further development. To achieve an effectiveness at the higher levels of society one must at some point give up adolescent patterns of sexuality and aggressivity and convert these powerful impulses into an energy that ramifies effectively into wider spheres of social, economic, and political life.

8. Sublimation. We now turn to the psychological mechanism that is involved in what I might call "salvation in the world." Sublimation is the mobilizing of a potentially destructive impulse and converting its energy into a culturally creative
manifestation. Sublimation involves the healthy adaptation to adverse circumstances, both within one's self and outside one's self. Certainly a dangerous energy is generated from the deprivation-frustration-hostility-aggression process. Yet, this energy can be used to do good for the individual and for the people who are members of his family or ethnic group. The performance of many socially accepted and valued roles can be the means of discharge of dangerous impulses. This involves the cultural shaping of motive forces in the form of values and rewards so that those human energies that derive from motivation are channelled into the common good.

Some examples can easily clarify this sublimation process. The impulse for direct physical aggression can be channelled in a number of positive directions. Boxing and other contact sports involving a high degree of aggression have been important avenues of social mobility for many persons at the bottom of the social ladder. The list of Black heroes in American athletics is legend, especially in boxing and football. Another social role that is open to those who need to express a great deal of aggression and which our society values highly is the role of the warrior, the soldier. It is in the performance of this role that one can engage in the act of homicide and be accepted, if not rewarded, for it. The police offers yet another culturally sanctioned and socially valued role for a more-or-less direct expression of physical aggression. Certainly the permission to carry an instrument of deadly force and to practice with it adds to the image of one's identity if one has those kinds of needs. The practice of medicine, with especial regard to the role of the surgeon, might be added to this list, although there are scarce few Black American practicianers of medicine to count among the members of the society of surgeons. Nevertheless, there is at least one study revealing high levels of hostility, in a few cases, pathologically high levels, among surgeons of high repute (personal communication with William Henry, University of Chicago), although no Black surgeons were represented.

Verbal aggression can be found sublimated in several general areas. Comedy gains much of its power from the expression of not-so-disguised hostility. Black comedy has had considerable impetus throughout the 1970's and appears to be normalizing in the 1980's. Verbal contests, commonly played in the streets of Black neighborhoods, are perennial modes of socialization within the peer group and include games like the dozens, as well as joning and signifying and general verbal manipulation. At a high level of verbal ability one can use aggressive energy in the practice of trial law. Here, especially in prosecution and cross-examination, one can find great satisfaction in defining one's self image as well as relieving one's self of taxing levels of hostility. And for those with a talent for writing, there is a wide field for personal expression through fiction, poetry, and drama, as well as the investigative realms of journalism and social science.

Revitalization movements. This is the last category of sublimation to be noted here. It is, in my opinion, by far the most important mode of sublimation to consider in the context of Black America. A revitalization movement involves the mobilization of a significant segment of a population and their organization into a body-politic sufficiently powerful to accomplish the common objectives of the group often against the resistance of a dominating power structure. Revitalization is a process that occurs within the individual and within the mobilized group. This process has a structure and a sequence of events that proceed along a path toward the realization of the group's goals. Aberle (1962) places the greatest importance for the motivation of these kinds of movements on relative deprivation and Wallace (1956) gives us an elegant conceptualization of the structure of this process. I shall proceed to delineate the revitalization model and use the Black Muslim movement (Essien-Udom, 1962; Parenti, 1964) as an illustration, although we could easily use the Black Power Movement or Martin Luther King's Civil Rights Movement as alternative examples.

Wallace defines a revitalization movement as "a deliberate, organized attempt to construct a more satisfying way of life with a rapid acceptance of new innovative life-styles" (1956, p. 265). A central concept is that of equilibrium. A stable society survives by maintaining some semblance of equilibrium, stability, routine. No society achieves perfect equilibrium but many societies, especially the more traditional societies, maintain a dynamic equilibrium through the balancing of opposing forces and successfully managing various levels of stress. Therefore, Wallace's first stage of the revitalization process is called the steady state. No society, not even the simplest societies, exists without change. So, by steady state we mean a slow, ordered sociocultural change with rises and falls in the levels of stress in the society, yet kept within the limits of tolerance and control. The "steady state" in Black history was the institution of slavery where "stability" was maintained under extreme coercion.

The second stage is called increased individual stress. This occurs when the society is increasingly pushed out of equilibrium by either some set of internal circumstances such as intolerable oppression or forces outside the society such as drought or invasion. At this stage the system is failing to

173

satisfy basic personal needs and the people attempt to cope
with a progressively intolerable stress. There follows a
widespread disillusionment in the system's ability to provide a
satisfying way of life and anomie, a breakdown in the meaning
and importance of basic values, prevails. At this point there
is a significant increase in sociopathic behavior, behavior that
violates the law, creates a danger to one's self and others,
and contributes to the deterioration of the existing fabric of
society. Nevertheless, an illusion of the steady state persists.
Persons see their trouble as their trouble and do not interpret
their state of affairs as a consequence of some societal
breakdown. To attempt to fit Black society into this category
may be forcing the issue since the real problem of stress was
that of the whole of American society.

   Stage three: The period of cultural distortion. At this
point in the development of the societal process many
members of the society attempt to restore their personal
equilibrium in pathological ways. As Wallace notes, these
attempts take the form of alcoholism, a growing venality of
public officials who are more interested in personal gain than
the public good, black market trading, breaches of kinship and
sexual mores including such acts as incest, adultery (where
the society professes faithful monogamy), progressive rise in
the divorce rate, and an increase in the public display of
homosexuality (in the society that declares such ways as
taboo). Hoarding, gambling for profit, and scapegoating
complete Wallace's list of examples. The important point of
this stage is that such behavior that was considered wrong,
illegal, or taboo at an earlier stage is now granted greater
acceptance and may even become institutionalized and legal in
the society. The elimination of prohibition, the legalization of
abortion and the decriminalization of the use of marijuana,
legal gambling in particular establishments, and legal
prostitution in certain counties of Nevada all serve as
examples of this phase of development. Rather than
attempting to wage a losing war against the so-called "evils"
of society, the government, in agreement with the public
consensus, turns the values and legal code around to accept

174

these modes of behavior and thus circumvent or neutralize these once immoral behaviors.

The fourth stage of the revitalization process, and that which is most directly relevant to our example of the Black Muslim movement, is the period of revitalization. Once severe cultural distortion gains momentum, society can either deteriorate further into a state of chaos, which happens from time to time, or it can, with great difficulty, pull itself together and reestablish a more satisfying way of life. Normally the inhabitants of a society experience prolonged periods of dissatisfaction and deprivation, if not outright misery, before they can get it together to change their condition either through slow directed change or through violent revolution.

Wallace's period of revitalization consists of six phases. The initiation of successive phases does not mean the previous phase has ceased to operate. As will be seen, the phases can easily operate simultaneously and even reinforce each other to a point. And then, the earliest phases wane in response to the gaining momentum of the latest phase, thus moving the process on to a point of maturation

The first phase in this process is the formulation of a code. The initiation of a movement requires an element of genius. It requires the atypical qualities of an individual to conceptualize a large amount of information and experience and put it all together in a way that generates the idea of a solution to a people's problem. This act of genius usually happens within the singular mind of an individual rather than the combined efforts of a group who hash out the problem. Although the latter group effort is vital to a movement, the original idea most often occurs as a very personal creative experience. This original idea need not spring "out of the blue" but may be a derivation of ideas and movements that occurred in earlier periods of history. Such is the case with the founder of the Nation of Islam in America, Elijah Muhammad. One remarkable predecessor was Marcus Garvey, the Jamaican Black separatist, who initiated what was to develop into the Rastafarian movement. Although the Black separatism notion was not new, the code of Islam applied to Black Americans was. The Islamic code was interpreted through the cultural framework and historical experience of Black culture and laid down as an alternative way of life. As Wallace describes it, the alternative ideology normally projects a utopian image and becomes a "blueprint for a new way of life."

The second phase of the revitalization period is communication. The word must be communicated. The new ideology must be preached and evangelized. Communication of the new ideology must accomplish several things. It must articulate the problem of the people in a way that mobilizes the sentiment for change. It must articulate the nature of the deprivations; it must express the anger born of those deprivations; it must offer a way out of the common problem; it must offer, if not promise, rewards for joining the movement. The aim of communication is to win converts. The rewards offered in the communication include material betterment, identification with a "superior" way of life, and a spiritual salvation.

The Black Muslim eschatology makes a simple and clear mythological explanation for the troubles of the Black people, maps out the path to liberation, and offers the promise of eternal salvation. This ideology itself has a likeness to our revitalization paradigm. The story goes that in the beginning one found a world sublime, for God (Allah) had created man who was Black. But, the devil came to the world in the form of Yakub, the white Evil Personage who is a direct opposition to Allah's peace and justice. Yakub and his white army overwhelmed and enslaved the Black man, which came to be known as the Fall. Great trouble and travail persisted until the Message was revealed. The Message came from Allah through the person of W.D. Fard who appeared in Detroit in the 1930's. It was Fard who brought Elijah Muhammad Allah's Word and it was Elijah Muhammad who gathered together his

Black people and went through their conversion as Black Muslims. It is the mission of the Nation of Islam to lead their people out of bondage into a separate nation that will enjoy a utopian existence within the autonomous Nation of Islam, and thus, redemption will be achieved. And vengence will be realized at Armageddon, when the wrath of Allah is wrought against the blue-eyed white devils who are no more than a corruption of humanity. And the Black man will henceforth rule the earth (Essien-Udom, pp. 122-142). Communication of the Word and the policies of the movement are carried by word of mouth in personal interactions, by preachings to the crowds of potential converts, through radio interviews, and by way of the official communicative organ of the movement, the newspaper, Muhammad Speaks.

The third phase of the revitalization period is called organization. This phase of the process is characterized by what I call the politicization of discontent. Conversion to Islam promises the satisfaction of basic needs and offers the paths to the realization of gaining what the white man has deprived the Black man. The barriers of relative deprivation are seen as superable--Elijah Muhammad promises his people that the barriers to the realization of what the others have can be shattered. The group gains converts and expands considerably to the point of necessitating an organizational structure. This structure has three levels. The charismatic leader at the top offers the Word and dictates the work. At a second level are the disciples who take his Word to the people, who, upon being converted, make up the third level, and who contribute service and money to the movement. The disciples become the executive branch of the organization. Their duties include responsibilities for organizing the program of evangelism, combatting any heresy that may develop within the ranks, and to protect the leader. Of course, the most notable heretic of this movement was the brilliant Malcom X, who, upon seeing the ideological flaws and the counter-exemplary behavior of his leader, took a new path, began developing a new ideology and innovative policy guidelines which resulted in his being cast out of the Nation of Islam.

177

The disciples, upon recruiting a sufficient number of members, can now leave their former ways of making a living and become full-time specialists, economically supported by the masses of followers. Organization does not end with setting up a structure of government. It also involves organizing the masses into a body of people who restructure their personal lives according to the Islamic codes of conduct.

The fourth phase of the period of revitalization Wallace calls adaptation. At this stage there is both an internal and an external challenge. The movement must certainly adapt itself to the sociopolitical environment of the larger society. It must keep from being too threatening to the dominant power structure of city or national government or face a possibly violent extinguishment as evidenced by the Black Panthers in Chicago. Further, the movement must adapt to internal strains, problems, and inadequacies. The ideology needs constant reworking in order to render it internally consistent, the social order needs to be kept under control so factions do not threaten the overall integrity of the movement and its goals, and the ideals must be kept alive and the promises reasserted in order to keep the people unified in motivation and orientation. Adaptation is a constant effort and has been the very viability of the Nation of Islam today, for it maintains a stable population of devotees.

This brings us to the fifth phase of the revitalization period, called cultural transformation. This is seen in the movement's ongoing stability and successful communication of the culture of the movement to the next generation. In this phase we find the successful working of institutions within the movement that function as adaptative units fostering continued structural organization. This is what Parenti (1964, p. 183) calls "organizational maturity and efficacy." A successful leadership and chain-of-command operates from the charismatic leader down "through his chief lieutenants to an aggressive and vigorous clergy" (Ibid.). The organization is endowed with a highly disciplined, emaculately dressed Fruit of Islam who act as a security force, often well-trained in the martial arts, guarding against threats from outside the temple and misbehavior within the temple. Each temple has stationed at least one member of the Fruit of Islam. There are also Temple Investigators who act as mediators for families burdened by discord, women's auxiliaries who teach domestic skills to the female youth, summer camps functioning as Muslim retreats for the youth, accredited grade schools, The University of Islam, that teaches the Black heritage, moral discipline, and the standard subjects required by state law. The movement also sponsors community centers, places of employment and job training, retail businesses, and housing agencies (Ibid.).

The last phase of the revitalization period is called routinization. Here we find usually an imperceptable shift from innovation to maintenance. This is accomplished through the process of institutionalization of the structures already in place. This means that there is no more questioning the significance of the structure. The structures and the social roles are valued and have legitimacy. Threats to these structures are responded to with sanctions against the member who acts in a threatening way. Probably the most important aspect of this phase is the fact that if the leader should die the movement would carry on, elect a new leader, and restabilize.

The adaptation of the movement is in place as we see that the integration into the larger society has not created any sustained conflicts. In fact, the morality of the Nation of Islam is hardly a contradiction to standard American values. As Parenti has stated,

> For all their virulent denunciation of the white man,
> the Muslims are assiduously modeling themselves after
> certain white middle-class ideals. Besides the
> interdiction on alcohol, tobacco and narcotics, the
> Muslim must refrain from gambling, fornicating,
> dancing, more than one daily meal, long vacations,
> idleness, excessive sleeping, lying, stealing, discourtesy
> (especially toward women), intemperate singing,

179

shouting or loud laughter....In addition, personal
cleanliness, the fastidious care of homes, thrift,
sobriety, diligent, honest work (even for a white
employer), and obedience to (white) civil authorities--
except on grounds of religious obligation --become
moral duties, while the middle-class dress of subdued
suit, tie and white collar becomes the Muslim uniform
(Ibid., p. 184).

For a period of time in the 1960's the ideology of the
movement directed less hostility toward the white man and
focused more
attention on the lower-class Black culture which exemplifies a
great deal of what the Muslim movement tries to eliminate
from the culture of Black Americans, most particularly, the
"slave mentality" of the ghetto Black which is seen as the
"enemy" of the Muslim movement. In the 1970's and 1980's
one finds a redirected hostility toward whites, with some
expression of antisemitism. The displacement function here
appears to have gained some impetus.

To follow Wallace's paradigm to its end, we find that this
last phase of the revitalization period ushers in the New
Steady State. The Muslim culture still fluctuates with the ebb
and flow and the stresses of the larger society and varies its
objectives according to the relative influences of its
leadership, but it has achieved a relative stability in American
society. As is the case in every human society and social
movement, this steady state becomes the initial stage of the
cycle in an ongoing, inexorable, evolutionary process of human
emergence.

PART IV

CONCLUSION

The study of Black culture, social organization, and personality involves a selective process that may be perplexing to an ethnographer studying any society. This is the process of selecting, out of a dizzying array of perceptions experienced by the fieldworker and a variety of descriptions from the literature, a body of data that provides a broad view of a people within an explanatory framework. The combination of data and theory create the experience of understanding not only for those who stand outside that group under study, but for those who are natives to that group as well, for the experience of one member is not the experience of all the members of the group, and the principles that are operating in the dynamics of the group are not so easily known from intuition. In this particular study I have attempted to utilize data that best documented the principles of social, cultural, and personality dynamics, and conversely, selected principles of social science theory that I felt best interpreted the ethnographic information brought to print by scientists and scholars.

My general orientation has been to place Black society into the evolutionary framework of the human species and then to show that those general principles that are operating within Black ethnicity apply to other groups as well and that the distinctive features of Black ethnicity emerge out of the unique historical, cultural, and social environments that have shaped Black ethnicity since the very beginnings of American society. Ethnographic studies that do not place the group into a larger framework often come out with a picture of an ethnic group that is very distinctive, clear cut, with well-formed boundaries around that cultural identity. This particular study blurs those lines of cultural identity because it brings out the fact that Blacks live as Americans in an American pluralistic society, and that because Black Americans are hardly isolated from other cultural and ethnic groups, they

181

share a great deal of the social and cultural life of others outside their own group.

This recognition of the overlap of sociocultural boundaries in a pluralistic society is commonsense, yet important, if only to underscore the necessity for ethnic integration in a pluralistic and democratic society. To put this notion in other words, the more unfamiliar one is with a particular ethnic group, the more that group will stand out in terms of stereotypes, over-generalizations, and even projections of one's own unacceptable traits that are impugned to the outgroup (the latter of which is an important psychological feature of racism). And, conversely, the closer one gets to a group and the more familiar one becomes with members of that group, the less will that group stand out as a stereotype or as a phantasmagoric configuration of images.

This process of recognition is also true for the ethnographer who often goes into a field situation in a remote area of the world with relatively little information to know or understand the people he or she is to be studying with. This is often a four-stage process. The first stage takes place completely outside the realm of the people to be investigated. The literature may have provided something of an ethnographic picture, but the people are not really understood as individuals in their continuous adaptation to their particular environment. They are known only in terms of generalizations made by previous travelers, missionaries, or ethnographers who, in their writings, created generalities, if not stereotypes, in the mind of the investigator who is about to embark on the study. The second stage occurs upon entering the realm of the people to be studied. The ethnographer is confronted with a dizzying array of stimuli and perceptions that, at first, creates disorientation, frustration, and confusion--some of the elements we recognize as culture shock. But, as time goes on the disparate perceptions begin to fall into place as the language is learned, as the ethnographer makes a personal adaptation to the physical and sociocultural environment, and as the natives of the group teach the ethnographer their ways. Then the third stage emerges as the ethnographer forges personal relationships in adapting to the day-to-day routines. Through this process of living with the natives of a different culture, becoming involved in relationships of interdependency, one's apperception of the boundaries of ethnicity recede, the culture becomes familiar, and the people become individuals as they are in one's own culture. The cultural differences have become minimized. As in one's own society there are people who become dear to the ethnographer, others who are strictly business associations, others who may even be enemies of one form or another, and the mass of people toward whom the ethnographer is relatively indifferent. It is at this stage that, every once in awhile, an ethnographer "gets lost" in the culture under investigation, becomes adopted by a family, marries one of that group, and/or makes the society a second home. The fourth stage is taking one's notes and memories back home and creating a written account of the experience and a scientific description and interpretation of the people. This latter stage can be prolonged, tedious, and difficult, yet punctuated by moments of illumination.

The problem of intercultural understanding and ethnic integration is one involving the light side and the dark side of a coin--the heads and the tails, respectively. The light side, heads, is that of intellectual understanding: For our purposes here it is the Black ethnic group's understanding of itself and the white ethnic groups' understanding and appreciation of Black ethnicity. The dark side of the coin, tails, is the realm of the unconscious, where lurks a variety of needs to hate and discriminate against an ethnic group labeled as society's scapegoat; scapegoat for all those frustrations, negative images of self, and needs that demand a target for the displacement of hostility and aggression in modes both subtle and violent.

In conclusion, the approach of this book has been to cast Black culture, social organization, and personality into the framework of a people's adaptation to historical, socio-political, and economic environments, all of which act as an

183

infrastructure in shaping those modes of adaptation that emerge as what we recognize today. Further, this work has stressed not only the distinctive features of Black ethnicity but also what all human beings share in common, due to our common evolutionary origins. Growing out of the species-specific human biological organism, similar principles of psychological functioning operate among members of all human groups. Those circumstances that are unique to the group give that group its distinctiveness just as those circumstances unique to an individual, give that person an induplicable personality. The creativity that is realized by an individual in solving a problem or expressing a sentiment and which is communicated to other members of the group gives that group its cultural distinctiveness, and in that way, makes a contribution to the wider society when members of that wider society begin to appreciate the quality of that contribution.

Although research on Black Americans has been going on for decades there is no less need for continued effort. America is a fast-changing society and the ethnic groups that make up the fabric of American society change more or less through time as well. There is still a great need to research the life of Black America since this segment of society is making considerable strides and going through great stresses of social change, the process of which must be documented. As the reader can easily see, this book has emphasized the poverty-level and working class level of Black society and has underemphasized middle and upper-middle class culture and social organization. As may be surmized, this work is reflecting the major areas of research and points out through implication that relatively little work has been done with the middle and upper-middle classes of Black America. This work needs the efforts of scholars both inside the Black ethnic group as well as outside it so that a dialogue may be continued on the human nature of Black ethnicity.

References

Aberle, David. 1962. A note on relative deprivation theory as
applied to millenarian and other cult movements. In
Millenarian dreams and action, Sylvia Thrupp, ed.,
Comparative studies in society and history, Supplement II,
pp. 209-214. The Hague: Mouton.

Abrahams, R. 1964. Deep down in the jungle: Negro
narrative folklore from the streets of Philadelphia.
Chicago: Aldine.

Aschenbrenner, J. 1975. Lifelines. New York: Holt,
Rinehart and Winston.

Barth, Frederik. 1969. Ethnic groups and boundaries: The
social organization of culture differences. Boston: Little
Brown.

Baugh, John. 1983. Black street speech. Austin: University
of Texas Press.

Bernstein, B. 1966. Elaborated and restricted codes: Their
social origins and some consequences. In The ethnography
of communication, J. Gumperz and Dell Hymes, eds.
Special publication, American Anthropologist, 66:6, Part 2.

Bott, Elizabeth. 1971. Family and social network. 2nd
Edition. New York: Free Press.

Brown, Claude. 1965. Manchild in the promised land. New
York: Signet Books.

Campbell, B.G. 1985. Humankind emerging. Boston: Little
Brown.

Cole, M. and J. Bruner. 1972. Cultural differences and
inferences about psychological processes. American
Psychologist, 26:867-876.

Cross, William. 1980. Models of negrescence: A literature
review. In Jones, ed., Black psychology, 81-98. New York:
Harper & Row.

Davis, Allison and John Dollard. 1940. Children of bondage. New York: Harper.

Dollard, John, Leonard W. Doob, Neal E. Miller, O.H. Mowrer, and Robert R. Sears. 1939. Frustration and aggression. New Haven: Yale University Press.

DuBois, W.E.B. 1903. The souls of Black folk. Chicago: A.C. McClurg & Co.

Eames, Edwin and Judith Goode. 1977. Anthropology of the city. Englewood Cliffs: Prentice-Hall.

Erikson, Erik H. 1963. Childhood and society, chapter 7. New York: W.W. Norton.

Essien-Udom, E.U. 1962. Black nationalism: A search for an identity in America. Chicago: University of Chicago Press.

Fauset, A.H. 1971. Black gods of the metropolis: Negro religious cults in the urban north. Philadelphia: University of Pennsylvania Press.

Frazier, E. Franklin. 1966. The Negro family in the United States. Chicago: University of Chicago Press.

Gardiner, James J. and J. Deotis Roberts, Sr., eds. 1971. Quest for a Black theology. Philadelphia: Pilgrim Press.

Geertz, Clifford. 1966. Religion as a cultural system. In Anthropological approaches to the study of religion. Michael Banton, ed. Association of Social Anthropologists Monograph #3. London: Tavistock.

Gwaltney, John Langston. 1980. Drylongso: A self-portrait of Black America. New York: Vintage Books.

Hamilton, W.D. 1964. The genetical evolution of social behavior. Journal of Theoretical Biology, 7:1-52.

Hannerz, Ulf. 1969. Soulside: Inquiries into ghetto culture and community. New York: Columbia University Press.

Hauser, Stuart T. 1971. Black and white identity formation. New York: John Wiley & Sons.

Herskovits, Melville. 1958. Myth of the Negro past. Boston: Beacon Press.

Jenkins, Adelbert H. 1982. The psychology of the Afro-American. New York: Pergamon.

Jones, Reginald. 1972. Black psychology (1st ed.). New York: Harper & Row.

----- ----- 1980. Black psychology (2nd ed.). New York: Harper & Row.

Kahn, Arnold. 1984. The power war: Male response to power loss under equality. Psychology of women quarterly, 8:3, 234-47.

Kennedy, Theodore. 1980. You gotta deal with it. New York: Oxford University Press.

Kochman, T. 1970. Towards an ethnography of Black speech behavior. In Afro-American Anthropology, N. Whitten and J. Szwed, eds. New York: Free Press.

Labov, William. 1972. Language in the inner city: Studies in the Black English vernacular. Philadelphia: University of Pennsylvania Press.

Leeds, Anthony. 1971. The concept of the 'culture of poverty': Conceptual, logical, and empirical problems with perspectives from Brazil and Peru. In E. Leacock, ed., Culture of poverty: A critique, pp. 226-84. New York: Simon and Schuster.

LeVine, Robert and Donald Campbell. 1972. Ethnocentrism: Theories of conflict, ethnic attitudes and group behavior. New York: John Wiley and Sons.

Lewis, Oscar. 1966. The culture of poverty. In Scientific American, 215 (4):19-25.

Liebow, Elliot. 1967. Tally's corner: A study of Negro streetcorner men. Boston: Little Brown.

Malcolm X. 1964. The autobiography of Malcolm X. New York: Grove Press.

Mangin, William, ed. 1970. Peasants in cities. Boston: Houghton Mifflin.

Maslow, Abraham. 1954. Motivation and personality. New York: Harper.

Mays, Benjamin Elijah and Joseph William Nicholson. 1969. The Negro's church. New York: Arno Press. Reprinted from the 1933 monograph The Negro's Church, Institute of Social and Religious Research.

McClelland, David, J.W. Atkinson, R.A. Clark, and E.L. Lowell. 1953. The achievement motive. New York: Appleton, Century, Crofts.

----- ----- 1975. Power: The inner experience. New York: John Wiley & Sons.

Miller, James G. 1978. Living systems. New York: McGraw Hill.

Miller, Walter. 1958. Lower class culture as a generating milieu of gang delinquency. In The sociology of crime and delinquency, Marvin E. Wolfgang, Leonard Savitz, and Norman Johnston, eds. New York: John Wiley & Sons.

Mitchell, Henry H. 1970. Black preaching. San Francisco: Harper and Row.

Nobles, Wade. 1972. African philosophy: Foundation for Black psychology. In Jones, ed., Black psychology (1st ed.), 18-32. New York: Harper & Row.

"Nothing But a Man." 1966. Ivan Dixson and Abbe Lincoln, principal actors. Sterling Films.

Parenti, Michael. 1964. The Black Muslims: From revolution to institution. Social Research, 31:175-194.

Parker, Seymour and R. Kleiner. 1972. The culture of poverty: An adjustive dimension. American Anthropologist, 72:516-28.

Parsons, Talcott and Robert Bales. 1955. Family, socialization and interaction process. Glencoe, Illinois: Free Press.

Reminick, Ronald A. 1983. Theory of ethnicity: An anthropologist's perspective. Lanham, Md.: University Press of America.

Rohrer, John H. and Munro S. Edmonson. 1960. The eighth generation grows up. New York: Harper.

Rosenfeld, Gerry. 1971. Shut those thick lips. New York: Holt, Rinehart, Winston.

Roberts, J. Deotis, Sr. 1971. Black consciousness in theological perspective. In Quest of a Black theology. Gardiner and Roberts, eds. Philadelphia: Pilgrim Press.

Safa, Helen. 1968. The social isolation of the urban poor:
   Life in a Puerto Rican shanty town. In I. Deutscher and
   E. Thompson, eds., Among the people: Encounters with the
   poor. New York: Basic Books.

Sapir, Edward. 1949. Culture, language, and personality:
   Selected essays. David Mandelbaum, ed. Berkeley:
   University of California Press.

Spiro, Melford. 1966. Religion: Problems of definition and
   explanation. In Anthropological approaches to the study of
   religion. Michael Banton, ed. Association of Social
   Anthropologists Monograph #3.

Stack, C. 1974. All our kin: Strategies for survival in a
   Black community. New York: Harper Colophon.

Staples, Robert. 1982. Black masculinity: The Black male's
   role in American society. San Francisco: The Black
   Scholar Press.

Symons, Donald. 1979. The evolution of human sexuality.
   New York: Oxford University Press.

Trivers, R.L. 1971. The evolution of reciprocal altruism.
   Quarterly Review of Biology, 46:35-57.

Valentine, Charles. 1968. Culture and poverty: A critique
   and counterproposals. Chicago: University of Chicago
   Press.

Washington, Joseph R. 1971. How Black is Black religion?
   In Gardiner and Roberts, ed., Quest for a Black theology.
   Philadelphia: Pilgrim Press.

Wallace, A.F.C. 1956. Revitalization movements. American
   Anthropologist, 58:264-281.

Wallace, A.F.C. 1961. Culture and personality. New York: Random House.

Weber, Max. 1947. The theory of economic and social organization. Talcott Parsons, ed. New York: Scribners.

White, Joseph L. 1984. The psychology of Blacks: An Afro-American perspective. Englewood Cliffs: Prentice-Hall.

Whiting, Beatrice B. 1965. Sex identity conflict and physical violence: A comparative study. American Anthropologist, 67:8, 123-140.

Whiting, John W.M. and Irvin Child. 1953. Child training and personality. New Haven: Yale University Press.

Williams, Melvin D. 1974. Community in a Black Pentecostal church. Prospect Heights, Illinois: Waveland Press.

Wilson, Amos N. 1978. The developmental psychology of the Black child. New York: Africana Research Publications.

Young, Virginia Heyer. 1974. A Black American socialization pattern. American Ethnologist, 1:2, pp. 405-413.

Index

formal 56
informal 56
endorphins 78
equilibrium 173, 174
ethnic boundaries 107
ethnic group 81, 88, 89, 98,
  100, 106-110
Evans-Pritchard, E.E. 21
evolution 37, 45
family
 blended 86
 extended 83, 88, 89, 92, 94,
  98, 99
 nuclear 82, 86-89, 98
Fauset, A.H. 101
fertility 93, 96
fictive kin 97, 99
field situation 26-28
fixation 152
foreclosure 153, 165
Frazier, E. Franklin 61
friendships 30
frustration-aggression 146,
  159, 160
gambling 57
Geertz, Clifford 66
Gwaltney, John 107
hair 58, 59
Hannerz, Ulf 22, 30, 93, 98
Harlem 126-129, 131-133, 135,
  137, 138
healing 72, 77, 78
Herskovits, Melville 60, 61
history 49-51, 55, 60, 61
impulsivity 166
inclusive fitness 16
informants 23, 27, 29
infrastructure 88
intra-sex competition 12

involution 167, 168
isolation 168, 169
kinesics 42
language 38, 39, 41, 42, 46
Leeds 63
LeVine, Robert, and Campbell,
  Donald 107
Lewis, Oscar 61-63
Liebow, Elliot 21, 22, 27, 98
locus
 ethnographic 21
 geographic 21, 22
macrocosmic 37
macrofields 5
maladaptation 10
Mangin, William 63
marriage 82, 84-87, 89, 91-94
masculine identity 84, 94
masculinity 97
material artifacts 58
matrifocal 88, 90, 91, 96, 97
Mays, Benjamin E., and
  Nicholson, Joseph W. 101
Mead, Margaret 21
microcosmic 37
microfields 6
migrations 100
Mitchell, Henry 68, 103-105
modus vivendi 27
modus operandi 26, 27
motherhood 92-94
music 71, 72, 77
music 54, 55, 58, 71, 72, 77
myth 66, 68, 69
mythology 68, 69
negritude 6
network analysis 22
nonverbal communication 41,
  42